Biological Warfare

by Don Nardo

THOMSON

---★---™

GALE

© 2007 Thomson Gale, a part of The Thomson Corporation.

Thomson and Star Logo are trademarks and Gale and Lucent Books are registered trademarks used herein under license.

For more information, contact
Lucent Books
27500 Drake Rd.
Farmington Hills, MI 48331-3535
Or you can visit our Internet site at http://www.gale.com

LIBRARY OF CONGRESS CATALOGING-IN-PUBLICATION DATA

Nardo, Don, 1947–
  Biological warfare / By Don Nardo.
    p. cm. — (Hot topics)
  " Discusses biological weapons, their development and use, and prevention of future use"—Publisher's summary.
  Includes bibliographical references and index.
  ISBN 1-59018-775-X (hardcover : alk. paper) 1. Biological warfare. 2. Biological weapons—Safety measures. 3. Bioterrorism—United States—Prevention. I. Title. II. Series: Hot topics (San Diego, Calif.)
UG447.8.N297 2006
358'.38—dc22
                                                            2006010020

Printed in the United States of America

CONTENTS

FOREWORD   4

INTRODUCTION   6
Biological Weapons: Knowledge, Intent,
    and Morality

CHAPTER ONE   11
Biological Agents and Their Harmful Effects

CHAPTER TWO   26
The Threat of Existing Bioweapons Programs

CHAPTER THREE   42
The Increasing and Daunting Threat
    of Bioterrorism

CHAPTER FOUR   58
Building Up Defenses Against Biological
    Attacks

CHAPTER FIVE   75
Preventing Future Biological Weapons
    Threats

NOTES   90

DISCUSSION QUESTIONS   94

FOR MORE INFORMATION   96

ORGANIZATIONS TO CONTACT   98

INDEX   100

PICTURE CREDITS   104

ABOUT THE AUTHOR   104

FOREWORD

Young people today are bombarded with information. Aside from traditional sources such as newspapers, television, and the radio, they are inundated with a nearly continuous stream of data from electronic media. They send and receive e-mails and instant messages, read and write online "blogs," participate in chat rooms and forums, and surf the Web for hours. This trend is likely to continue. As Patricia Senn Breivik, the dean of university libraries at Wayne State University in Detroit, states, "Information overload will only increase in the future. By 2020, for example, the available body of information is expected to double every 73 days! How will these students find the information they need in this coming tidal wave of information?"

Ironically, this overabundance of information can actually impede efforts to understand complex issues. Whether the topic is abortion, the death penalty, gay rights, or obesity, the deluge of fact and opinion that floods the print and electronic media is overwhelming. The news media report the results of polls and studies that contradict one another. Cable news shows, talk radio programs, and newspaper editorials promote narrow viewpoints and omit facts that challenge their own political biases. The World Wide Web is an electronic minefield where legitimate scholars compete with the postings of ordinary citizens who may or may not be well-informed or capable of reasoned argument. At times, strongly worded testimonials and opinion pieces both in print and electronic media are presented as factual accounts.

Conflicting quotes and statistics can confuse even the most diligent researchers. A good example of this is the question of whether or not the death penalty deters crime. For instance, one study found that murders decreased by nearly one-third when the death penalty was reinstated in New York in 1995.

Death penalty supporters cite this finding to support their argument that the existence of the death penalty deters criminals from committing murder. However, another study found that states without the death penalty have murder rates below the national average. This study is cited by opponents of capital punishment, who reject the claim that the death penalty deters murder. Students need context and clear, informed discussion if they are to think critically and make informed decisions.

The Hot Topics series is designed to help young people wade through the glut of fact, opinion, and rhetoric so that they can think critically about controversial issues. Only by reading and thinking critically will they be able to formulate a viewpoint that is not simply the parroted views of others. Each volume of the series focuses on one of today's most pressing social issues and provides a balanced overview of the topic. Carefully crafted narrative, fully documented primary and secondary source quotes, informative sidebars, and study questions all provide excellent starting points for research and discussion. Full-color photographs and charts enhance all volumes in the series. With its many useful features, the Hot Topics series is a valuable resource for young people struggling to understand the pressing issues of the modern era.

INTRODUCTION

BIOLOGICAL WEAPONS: KNOWLEDGE, INTENT, AND MORALITY

The threat of biological, or germ, warfare is not new, but has existed throughout history. To name only two of many examples, some medieval armies catapulted bodies infected with bubonic plague—the so-called Black Death—into enemy fortresses and towns, hoping to infect the inhabitants. And in the eighteenth century groups of Europeans purposely infected Native Americans with smallpox, a disease to which the natives had no resistance. Thousands died horribly as a result.

Yet as bad as these attacks were, they pale in comparison with those possible today. In fact, the threat of germ warfare is now far greater than it has ever been. This is partly because of advances in human knowledge, particularly about microbiology (the study of microbes, or germs), in the past century and a half. Biological attacks in past ages were isolated and localized events. More importantly, the attackers did not understand exactly how their primitive bioweapons worked, since germs were not discovered until the late nineteenth century. Had these early biological warriors understood the true nature of germs and how to culture them in a lab, they could have inflicted much more death and misery.

Knowledge

Today, in contrast, even most small children have a basic understanding about germs and a young adult with even a rudimentary education can easily use libraries and the Internet to learn about how to use germs as weapons. Such a person could then launch a bioterror attack; in fact, such attacks occurred periodically on a small scale between 1972 and 2001. The knowledge that made these events possible is available because a number of countries, including the United States, the Soviet Union, Germany, Britain, and Japan, developed biological warfare programs in the twentieth century. Though most countries have signed international treaties banning such weapons, experts warn that some nations may still maintain secret stockpiles. Thus the potential now exists for nation-states or individual terrorists to launch large-scale biological attacks that could kill tens of thousands or even millions of people.

U.S. soldiers check radiation levels during a biological warfare exercise.

Intent

Yet having the ability to use biological weapons is one thing, and actually using them is quite another. The fact that so many countries conceived of and signed international bans on such weapons shows that in general, organized societies do not have a strong intent to use them. These societies are ultimately made up of communities of families. And expert observers point out that the members of most families, no matter where they live on the globe, view dangerous germs as enemies to be fought and eradicated rather than as allies to be exploited. As Rutgers University scholar Leonard A. Cole points out:

> Everyone experiences bacterial and viral infections. . . . Whether debilitation from infection is slight or severe, every person has an intimate sense of the power of unfriendly germs. . . . The words we use to describe our relation to disease are common in any military training manual. Bacteria "attack." We are "fighting" a "war" on cancer. . . . A virus "overwhelms" our "defenses."[1]

Morality

Most people across the world, therefore, have no serious intent to use biological weapons. Some experts go further and contend that the general fear of and repugnance toward disease germs makes the use of such weapons appear immoral to most people. In fact, this moral sense, Cole suggests, "is the justification for [the existing] international rules, norms, and punishments that discourage biological warfare."[2]

That does not mean, however, that isolated individuals or groups, or even an occasional rogue nation, will not deviate from the norm. A handful of horrifying events in recent years have brought home the reality that such entities pose a real and present danger to civilized societies everywhere. These events include the 1993 attack on the World Trade Center in New York, which killed six and injured more than a thousand; the destruction of a federal building in Oklahoma City in 1995 by American extremist Timothy McVeigh, an act that killed 168

Police officers help a woman flee the World Trade Center after it was bombed in 1993. Events like this one are a reminder of what some groups will do.

people; and the 9/11 attacks in 2001, in which members of the terrorist group al Qaeda, headed by Osama bin Laden, killed some three thousand people.

Clearly, a sense of morality, at least as the vast majority of people in the world would define it, was lacking in all of these attackers. In the words of terrorism expert Jim A. Davis:

> We can look to the emergence of organizations such as Al Quaeda . . . and see that previous moral constraints for massive civilian deaths are no longer applicable. They have launched a "holy war" against the United States and are not [reluctant] to inflict heavy casualties on U.S. citizens.[3]

In fact, Davis points out, Bin Laden and other terrorist leaders have actually claimed that their attacks are moral within the framework of their own personal religious and political beliefs. In this way, the concept of morality has been used both to ban and to justify the use of weapons of mass destruction.

A Daunting Challenge

Davis and other experts say that among such weapons, which include conventional bombs, biological and chemical agents, and nuclear weapons, biological agents are fast emerging as weapons of choice for would-be attackers. This is partly because some bioweapons require relatively little expert knowledge, money, and time to create. Supplementing this disturbing fact is the strong intent by a few to use such weapons. Experts warn that the resulting equation will pose a truly daunting challenge to civilization as a whole in the early decades of the twenty-first century.

BIOLOGICAL AGENTS AND THEIR HARMFUL EFFECTS

The term *biological agent* has become increasingly familiar to members of the general public in recent years. In large part this is because stories about weapons of mass destruction, including biological weapons, are mentioned often in national and even local television newscasts. Television documentaries, newspaper and magazine articles, and school classrooms are other venues in which these weapons are periodically mentioned or discussed.

Scientists and other experts define biological agents as diseases or toxins (poisons) that can potentially be used in biological warfare or bioterrorism. At present, these experts recognize more than twelve hundred biological agents. Some are microorganisms (germs), such as bacteria, viruses, and microscopic fungi and algae; others are tiny parasites; and still others are the toxins given off by some of these organisms.

Most of these agents exist, and have long existed, in varying amounts in nature. Usually, when a person encounters one of them in very small doses, it does little or no harm. One of the more familiar biological agents, *Bacillus anthracis*, better known as anthrax, for example, is harmless in tiny quantities. In fact, tens of thousands of people come into contact with a few anthrax spores in their home or workplace every day and suffer no ill effects. In more potent doses, however, when larger numbers of spores are present, an exposed animal or person can become very sick or even die.

People who plan to engage in biological warfare or bioterrorism take advantage of this simple fact of nature. They seek ways of isolating, concentrating, and/or growing biological agents in sufficient quantities to make them harmful to other people. Turning an existing natural germ or other substance into a weapon is often referred to as weaponizing it. Some biological agents are fairly easy and inexpensive to weaponize, whereas others require a great deal of expertise and money to make them a viable threat to human populations.

Thus a person or group planning a biological attack must take into account two major factors. First, the agent chosen must be debilitating or lethal in concentrated doses. But second, and just as important, the agent must be weaponizable using a reasonable amount of time, money, and effort; otherwise, turning the potential agent into an effective weapon is beyond the logistical capabilities of the would-be attacker.

Anthrax, seen here under a microscope, can be deadly in large doses and is inexpensive to make into a weapon.

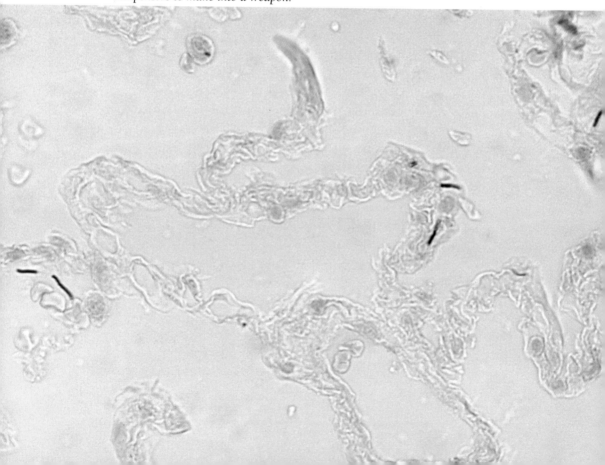

At present, experts recognize fourteen biological agents that are both potentially lethal and readily weaponizable for use against human populations. Besides anthrax, some of the more dangerous and frightening agents in this group are smallpox, botulinum toxin, bubonic plague, Q fever, and ricin. In addition, certain animal diseases, notably foot-and-mouth disease (FMD), could potentially be used to conduct agrowarfare or agroterrorism. Agrowarfare is a form of biological warfare designed to reduce or destroy a community's or a nation's food supply by killing its livestock. Yet nearly all biological agents have the potential for harm.

Anthrax a Weapon of Choice?

Anthrax is probably the most familiar and feared biological agent today. In part this is because of the national scare that occurred shortly after the attacks on the World Trade Center and the Pentagon in September 2001—the 9/11 attacks. A number of reporters, legislators, and other people received small but lethal concentrations of anthrax spores in mailed envelopes and at least five people died. The culprits are still unidentified.

Although this was the first time anthrax captured national attention in the United States, as well as in other countries, the disease itself is far from new. For centuries, naturally produced anthrax has killed cattle, sheep, and other livestock, as well as occasionally a few humans. No one knew what caused the disease or how it spread until 1876, when German researcher Robert Koch discovered irrefutable evidence for what came to be known as the anthrax disease cycle. The cycle begins with the anthrax germs, which are a type of bacteria. After the anthrax germs infect an animal, many of them change into spores and some of these spores enter the soil. The spores are tough and resistant to extremes in temperature, so they can remain in the soil for months or even years, lying dormant until a healthy animal happens by and eats some grass or other vegetation in the infected area. In this way, the spores enter the animal's warm blood. There they spring to life, reproduce, infect the host, and finally revert to spore form, beginning the cycle once again.

Anthrax spores can also pass from an infected animal to a human being. Most naturally occurring human cases of anthrax

How Anthrax Spreads

Anthrax causes flu-like symptoms, breathing difficulty, and skin lesions.

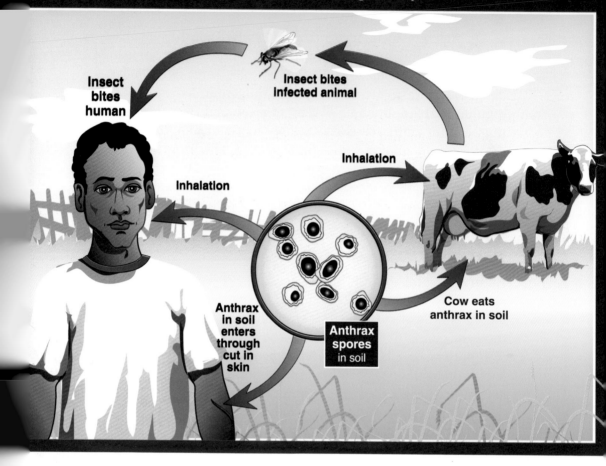

Insect bites human

Insect bites Infected animal

Inhalation

Inhalation

Anthrax in soil enters through cut in skin

Anthrax spores in soil

Cow eats anthrax in soil

have been among farmers and other people who come into regular, close contact with livestock. In the vast majority of these cases, the person catches the disease when spores enter the bloodstream through a cut or abrasion, a form of transmission called cutaneous. Only a few people have contracted pulmonary anthrax, in which the spores directly enter the lungs. As biological warfare expert Eric Croddy explains:

> Of those who get infected with cutaneous anthrax . . . 10 to 20 percent are likely to die if the disease is left untreated. For pulmonary, or inhalation, anthrax, the rate is much higher. This form of the disease occurs when an individual breathes in thousands of spores and develops an infection that begins in the lungs. Left untreated,

some 90 to 100 percent of people who contract inhalation anthrax may die.[4]

In the early years of the twentieth century, people in some countries, notably Germany and Japan, saw the potential for using concentrated anthrax spores as a weapon. Later, the United States, the Soviet Union, and other nations also conducted experiments

Human Signs of Cutaneous Anthrax

Anthrax spores are a weapon of choice for both national biological weapons producers and bioterrorists. An expert on biological agents here lists the symptoms of anthrax when it results from the spores making contact with a person's skin.

In humans, an anthrax infection can begin in one of three ways. Infection through the skin (cutaneous anthrax) is . . . the most common and obvious form. It begins with a tiny pimple. In a few hours this eruption becomes a reddish-brown irritation and swelling that turns into an ulcer . . . that splits the skin. The black scablike crust that the lesion develops gives the disease its name, *anthracis*, the Latin transliteration of the Greek word for coal. . . . Without treatment, the fatality rate for cutaneous anthrax can be 20 percent.

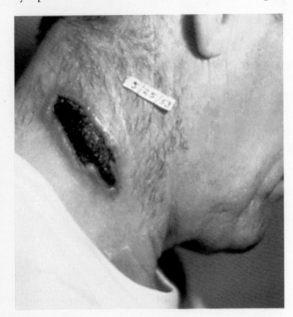

The black crust of an anthrax lesion shows through a large break in the skin.

Jeanne Guillemin, *Anthrax: The Investigation of a Deadly Outbreak*. Berkeley and Los Angeles: University of California Press, 1999, p. 4.

in weaponizing anthrax. And more recently, terrorists, including the unknown attacker in 2001, have begun to use the spores against other people. In fact, some experts fear that because of its fairly easy availability in nature, anthrax may become a weapon of choice for many bioterrorists.

Lethal Spores

The airborne anthrax spores are inhaled and lodge in the lungs. There, they quickly multiply and produce toxins that spread through the body via the bloodstream. One billionth of a gram can kill one person.

E.J. Gong, "The Invisible Weapons," *Defence Journal*, October 1998. www.defence journal. com/oct98/invisible_weapons.htm.

Fortunately, however, anthrax is generally not contagious from person to person, as are the flu and tuberculosis. Thus, an army soldier or terrorist wielding weaponized anthrax spores can kill only as many people as he or she can directly expose to the spores. It is also fortunate that anthrax can be successfully treated with antibiotics in the early stages of an infection. The bad news, as Croddy puts it, is that infected people "may not know they are infected until they are well into the course of the infection. This is a very serious problem because anthrax needs to be treated quickly."[5]

Smallpox Could Spread Across the Globe in Days

Another biological agent that experts worry about is one of the most dreaded diseases in history—smallpox. Among the characteristic symptoms of smallpox are high fever, chills, pain, eruptions of pus-filled sores (the so-called pox), and quite often death. Unlike anthrax, smallpox is caused by a virus rather than a bacterium. Also unlike anthrax, smallpox is mainly a disease of humans, rather than animals, and is highly contagious. The disease "spreads person to person," medical expert Brenda J. McEleney writes,

via inhalation of [tiny] water droplets . . . exhaled by infected individuals. However, as with common cold viruses, the smallpox virus can be introduced into the human body by touching a contaminated object, then subsequently touching one's nose or mouth with the contaminated hand. . . . There are two principal forms of the virus—variola major and a milder form, variola minor.[6]

Because it produces much more serious symptoms than the milder kind of smallpox, variola major has caused most of the millions of smallpox deaths that have occurred over the centuries. Indeed, for thousands of years the disease has spread through towns and countries around the world, leaving a trail of misery and death. So many people died when the disease struck ancient Rome, for instance, that there were not enough wagons to carry the dead out of the city. In desperation, the survivors threw thousands of corpses into the nearby Tiber River. Over the centuries, other outbreaks of smallpox wiped out hundreds of thousands of people in China, Europe, and Central America.

Thanks to a vaccine developed by a nineteenth-century doctor named Edward Jenner, the death toll from smallpox began to decrease dramatically in the 1800s. Over time, the governments of

most industrialized countries initiated programs to vaccinate most of their inhabitants. However, in less-developed nations poverty and inadequate medical facilities frequently prevented large-scale vaccination programs. Thus, even as late as the year 1967, 10 million cases of the disease, about one-fifth of them fatal, were reported worldwide.

Disturbed by these figures, in the late 1960s the World Health Organization (WHO), an agency of the United Nations, decided to try to eradicate smallpox once and for all. The agency dispatched hundreds of teams of doctors to vaccinate people whenever and wherever outbreaks of the illness were re-

Pus-filled sores caused by smallpox cover this man's face and body.

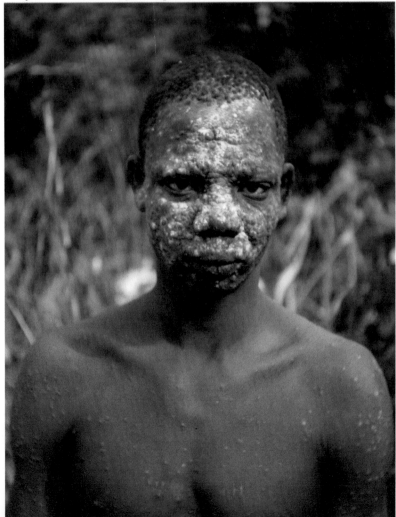

ported. Thanks to this concerted effort, success came with astounding swiftness. In October 1977 the last known case of the disease was reported in Africa, and WHO proudly declared that smallpox had been eliminated.

In reality, however, smallpox had been eliminated only from human populations. Scientists had kept cultures of the disease intact in laboratories around the world, saying it was vital to keep these samples for future research. Eventually, all of these samples were supposedly collected and stored in two labs, one in the United States, the other in Russia. Some people fear, however, that one or more sample smallpox cultures may have been secretly stored elsewhere, perhaps in rogue nations. Rogue nations are countries that are widely seen as subverting or ignoring international law and posing a danger to world peace.

Another worry voiced by some experts is that one of the known samples of the disease might fall into the wrong hands. They warn that a terrorist group in possession of such a sample and the means of culturing it could wreak terrible devastation on humanity. Recent studies have revealed that more than 40 percent of Americans have never received a smallpox vaccination. Moreover, some evidence suggests that the vaccinations administered to people decades ago may have lost much of their effectiveness. Thus, McEleny points out, "a release of smallpox would be cause for worldwide alarm." People traveling on airplanes and trains "could unknowingly spread the virus around the world within days," she says. "Healthcare systems would be overwhelmed if an outbreak were not contained early."[7]

A Deadly Bacterium and a Lethal Toxin

Although anthrax and smallpox would definitely be weapons of choice for those nations or independent terror groups with the ability to weaponize them, several other substances could potentially be used as biological agents. Of these, the most well known is bubonic plague. Caused by the bacterium *Yersinia pestis*, the plague has repeatedly devastated human communities throughout recorded history. The worst outbreak was in the 1300s, when the disease wiped out an estimated one-third of Europe's population in only a few years.

For a long time people were almost helpless to combat the plague because they did not know about the existence of germs. Finally, in the 1890s, biologists correctly identified the disease and determined how it spread. First, the bacteria multiply rapidly in the bloodstream of an infected animal, most often a rodent. Fleas that normally infest rodents then bite the animals and ingest the deadly germs. Although these insects usually remain in the host's fur, if the infected rodent comes into close contact with people, one or more fleas can transfer to a human host. When the fleas bite the person, the bacteria enter that person's bloodstream and he or she contracts the disease. These germs move through the lymphatic system to the lymph nodes and there multiply, forming large colonies. Within three to eight days, the resultant swelling creates the egg-shaped lumps, or buboes, that characterize the disease, usually in the groin or underarms. After another three or four days, the bacteria reach the bloodstream and move to the vital organs, especially the spleen and lungs. There, dark spots form, a process that long ago gave the plague its familiar nickname the Black Death. Finally, the victim suffers bleeding from the skin, bleeding from the bowels, and in most cases, if untreated, death.

Bubonic plague can be treated with antibiotics when caught in its early stages. Also, like HIV, the virus that causes AIDS, the plague bacterium does not normally pass from human to human except in rare cases. For instance, if the disease infects the lungs with a variant called pneumonic plague, it can be passed to another person if he or she inhales tiny respiratory droplets expelled by the infected person. Because pneumonic plague is extremely rare, however, under normal conditions the disease does not spread unless a lot of infected fleas are present.

Botulinum Toxin

Thus, at first glance it would seem that someone who wanted to use the disease as a weapon would need to gather up large numbers of infected fleas and unleash them on a human community. Experts on biological warfare say this would be very difficult to do and would likely end up killing relatively few people. The experts warn that today a sophisticated terrorist would more likely try to place a lot of plague bacteria in an aerosol container. That way he or she

A painting depicts the suffering and death caused by a bubonic plague epidemic in Europe in the 1300s.

could spray the microscopic germs into the air in a crowded section of a city. This could create a situation similar to pneumonic plague, and many unsuspecting people might breathe in the bacteria and contract the disease.

Another substance that has killed people on a periodic basis throughout recorded history is a lethal poison known as the botulinum toxin, which causes botulism. Botulism is a serious condition acquired by ingesting spoiled meat. The culprit behind the spoilage is a bacterium called *Clostridium botulinum*, which itself is not dangerous to animals or people. Instead, when these bacteria die and begin to decompose, they release the toxin, consisting of a tiny glob of protein, as a by-product.

What makes the botulinum toxin attractive to would-be biological attackers is its extreme lethality. It is among the most poisonous substances known; even a microscopic quantity is one hundred thousand times more dangerous than a dose of nerve gas and can quickly kill a human. Within twenty-four hours of ingesting a sufficient amount of the toxin, a person would die of respiratory failure.

No Danger

One anthrax spore, even thousands of spores, will not kill anyone. Wool sorters inhale 150 to 700 anthrax spores per hour continually without danger.

Steven Milloy, "Anthrax a Weapon of Mass Terrorism?" *Cato Commentary*, October 18, 2001.

Of course, poisoning a lot of meat and then trying to get large numbers of people to eat it would obviously be very awkward and would likely end up killing only a few people. As in the case of plague, experts say, the more efficient approach would be to find some way of getting the toxin into an aerosol spray. The toxin could also be poured into a city's water supply. "If a city's water purification system were blocked," Cole points out,

a gallon of botulinum toxin in the water system could theoretically kill millions [of people]. An innocent-looking fishing boat might encircle Manhattan Island, blowing [the toxin] from an inconspicuous aerosol generator. Again, casualties could be in the millions. The boat and all traces of its activities would long be gone before the massive outbreak of [sickness] was apparent.[8]

Some Agents Easy to Produce

One of the factors that makes bubonic plague and botulinum toxin highly feasible for and attractive to would-be attackers is that they are relatively easy to produce. A small makeshift lab in someone's garage or basement could potentially create large quantities of these substances over time. The same is true of another dangerous biological agent, Q fever. Scientists gave it this name, in which the Q stands for *query*, because at first they had difficulty understanding it and how it works. Q fever is caused by rickettsiae, microorganisms that share certain characteristics of both bacteria and viruses. The Q fever rickettsiae can be found in small amounts on some farms and in some slaughter-houses and farmers and butchers are normally the most likely individuals to contract the disease.

However, Q fever can easily be created in larger amounts by culturing the microbes in chicken eggs. Many billions of rick-ettsiae could be produced in a single egg. The germs could then be weaponized, like many other biological agents, by placing them in an aerosol sprayer.

Few people would die during a purposeful Q fever release, mainly because the disease is rarely fatal. However, victims do become quite sick, and such an attack could cause widespread fear and panic in a given city or society.

Two other biological agents that could be produced in a fairly small and unsophisticated lab are ricin and saxitoxin. Both consist of proteins that are highly poisonous to humans. Ricin can be extracted from the castor plant using relatively

Water supplies in large cities such as New York (pictured) and small cities could be easily contaminated with toxins.

simple laboratory procedures. This naturally makes it tempting to would-be biological attackers. Experts say ricin is difficult to weaponize but point out that an individual or group with sufficient time, money, and resources could do it. "Ricin is considered a real threat," Croddy writes, "and research continues in the United States to develop treatment and [a] vaccine for it."[9]

Saxitoxin could be even more deadly than ricin if effectively weaponized and unleashed by attackers. Saxitoxin derives from microscopic algae found in the oceans. When enough of these germs come together in one area, they form a so-called red tide, which infects local shellfish; when someone eats the shellfish he or she can die in two to twelve hours if the illness is not recognized and treated. The toxin can easily be grown in a lab. Moreover, someone could place a large concentration of the toxin in a bomb and explode it in a crowded area. Some of the toxin would then become airborne and people would breathe it in.

Still another easy-to-make biological agent is foot-and-mouth disease, the world's most contagious and dangerous animal disease. This virus, which causes blisters, lameness, and often death in the

Ricin can be extracted from castor beans (pictured). Though it is difficult to make into a weapon, ricin is considered to be a real threat.

Unleashing an Animal Epidemic

Growing cultures of foot-and-mouth disease and spreading the germs among a nation's livestock would not be difficult for a determined person, experts point out. The following is one suggested scenario:

A terrorist arrives in the nation's capital armed with a weapon obtained from the blistered tongue of an African cow with . . . foot-and-mouth disease. With several million particles of virus stored in a lunch cooler, he rents a car at Dulles International Airport outside Washington [D.C.] and drives south into the Virginia countryside. At several farms, he stops where cows or horses stand near fences and, using wads of cotton, calmly rubs some of the virus into their nostrils. By the time he reaches Richmond, an epidemic is virtually assured.

Steve Goldstein, "U.S. Officials Awakening to Threat of Agro-Terror," *Dallas Morning News,* June 27, 1999.

victim, remains a serious naturally occurring problem in more than thirty countries. A would-be attacker who wants to spread fear and/or inflict economic damage on a target could wipe out large numbers of a nation's livestock, including cattle, sheep, goats, and pigs. "A terrorist could travel to any one of the . . . countries in which foot-and-mouth disease is endemic," bioterrorism expert Michael E. Peterson points out. The person could then "purchase an infected animal and with a rudimentary knowledge of microbiology, obtain a sample . . . for intentional introduction into our herds."[10]

Anthrax, smallpox, bubonic plague, botulinum toxin, Q fever, ricin, saxitoxin, and foot-and-mouth disease are only a few of the biological agents that could be extremely dangerous in the wrong hands. There are many others. Clearly, therefore, many avenues for biological warfare exist. The burning questions are: Which of these avenues will be used most often? And will it be nation-states or terrorist groups that end up employing them?

THE THREAT OF EXISTING BIOWEAPONS PROGRAMS

Since the 9/11 attacks in New York City and Washington, D.C., in 2001 and the anthrax attacks that followed in their wake, the Western media have focused a great deal of attention on the threat of terrorism, including bioterrorism. Experts in biological warfare say that worries about the threat of bioterrorism are certainly justified. However, they caution that the emphasis on terrorism may presently be drawing too much attention away from a biological threat just as big as the terrorist one: the continuing development of bioweapons programs by sovereign nations. The experts often refer to such efforts undertaken by nation-states as state-sponsored programs.

State-sponsored biological warfare projects were condemned and largely banned by international conventions in the twentieth century. Yet many experts believe that such programs still exist in some countries, including the United States, Russia, and China, as well as in some so-called rogue states. In fact, public officials in the United States readily admit that the government has stepped up research into biological agents since the 2001 attacks. At least twenty labs around the country are engaged in such research and there are plans to build at least twenty more. Government spokesmen claim that these facilities are and will be used only to look for ways of defending the U.S. citizenry against foreign biological attacks; the labs will not try to manufacture offensive biological weapons, they say.

However, some individuals and organizations have voiced concerns that these programs might be used to make weapons in the future, in violation of international agreements. Moreover, they worry that the labs, many of which are located in densely populated areas, are a potential danger to the public. Accidents might occur, critics warn, that could kill large numbers of people in surrounding communities. "The work in these laboratories is exceedingly dangerous to the scientists," say investigators Dee Ann Divis and Nicholas M. Horrock,

> and potentially deadly to vast numbers of the population if the microbes were to get to the outside. Since most of the most lethal potential agents can be distributed through the air, the main approach to safety is preventing the germs and viruses from leaking out of the secure containers and rooms where scientists work with them.[11]

A technician works with a virus at a lab in Maryland. Research on biological agents in the United States has increased since the 2001 terrorist attacks.

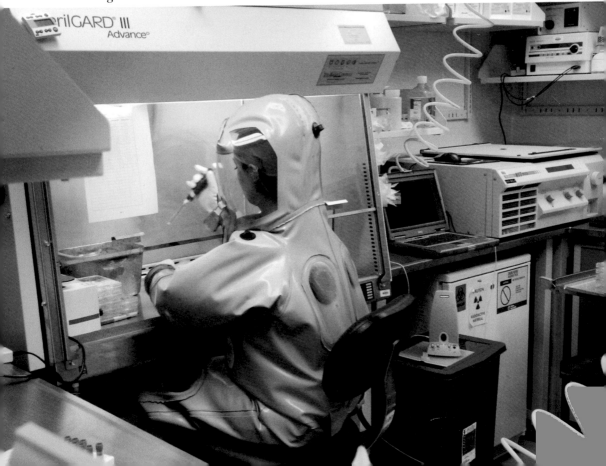

In the meantime, even more worrisome to most biowarfare experts is the potential danger posed by older state-sponsored research programs. In particular, there are fears that stockpiles of old bioweapons and/or detailed blueprints for making more of them still exist in some countries. The nation mentioned most often in this regard is the former Soviet Union, which is now Russia, Ukraine, and several other sovereign countries. A real threat exists, the experts say, that such stockpiles or blueprints could be secretly sold to or stolen by terrorists or agents working for rogue states, or even small countries not viewed as rogue states. These dangerous materials could be very valuable to such states because they could be used as the foundations of bioweapons development programs.

The Development of State-Sponsored Bioweapons Programs

These current worries about ongoing state-sponsored biological warfare efforts are based on the realities of the bioweapons programs that came into being in the twentieth century. In the early 1900s, as the new science of microbiology progressed rapidly, a number of scientists and government officials in various countries recognized the potential of germs as weapons. As time went on, state-sponsored research into biological weapons was kept secret because no country wanted to be accused of conducting research into weapons widely viewed as inhumane.

Yet this research did continue, at first mainly in richer industrialized countries that could afford to fund the scientists and expensive labs required. Germany was an early leader in this work. During World War I, U.S. and British officials accused the Germans of developing biological weapons. Proof later emerged that the Germans had infected horses with anthrax and let them loose in France, hoping they would spread the disease to French animals. German researchers also infected sheep with anthrax and planned to let them loose in Russia.

Though the Russians (by this time called Soviets) condemned the German biological warfare programs, they were

Grisly Tests on Human Subjects

Although many nations have studied and experimented with biological weapons in recent times, most of these programs have been secret and their details rarely come to light. One exception is Japan's biological warfare program, the details of which emerged after that nation's defeat in World War II. Allied investigators discovered that Japanese leaders had launched what they called Unit 731 in a facility located in a remote area of Manchuria, which the Japanese had recently taken from the Chinese. About three thousand scientists and technicians worked at the complex, which studied anthrax, cholera, bubonic plague, typhus, tetanus, small-pox, botulinum toxin, tick encephalitis, and tuberculosis. The labs in the complex were able to produce up to eight tons of bacteria per month. The researchers also conducted tests on human subjects, mostly prisoners of war, including Chinese, British, Americans, and Australians. In one test, the prisoners were given food containing cultures of botulism to see how long it would take them to die. In another gruesome experiment, prisoners were tied to stakes and exposed to a bomb containing gas gangrene germs. The Japanese also injected test subjects with anthrax, cholera, bubonic plague, and many other diseases.

soon engaged in similar programs that eventually far outstripped anything Germany had produced. The Soviet experiments in the following decades were dangerous in two ways, the most obvious being that the weapons produced posed a threat to other nations. The Soviet bioweapons programs also showed clearly that unanticipated accidents can occur during such research. In 1941, for example, the Soviets conducted biological experiments on political prisoners in Mongolia. Some of the victims were placed in cells with rats infested with fleas carrying bubonic plague germs. The prisoners contracted the disease. Then some of them, still infested with fleas, escaped and infected the residents of some nearby Mongolian villages. Within a few weeks, an estimated four to five thousand people died of the plague.

Another Soviet bioweapons accident took place in 1979. A secret biological warfare facility in the town of Sverdlovsk accidentally released deadly anthrax spores that had been weaponized in an aerosol spray. The spray traveled downwind to the town and infected ninety-four people. Sixty-four of them died within six weeks, and livestock located up to 30 miles (48.3km) from the leak were also infected. Though the Soviet Union no longer exists, Russian authorities continue to restrict access to the facility by foreign inspectors and reporters.

Vulnerable to Terrorism

Some experts worry that the countries of the former Soviet Union, with enormous stockpiles of pathogens, high levels of corruption, and grim conditions for scientists, could be vulnerable to terrorists.

Fred Guterl and Eve Conant, "In the Germ Labs," *Newsweek*, February 25, 2002.

In the meantime, the Americans, who had long condemned the German and Soviet bioweapons programs, were secretly developing their own. In the 1940s the U.S. government spent more than $40 million on biological weapons research. A large portion of this money went into building a weapons plant in Vigo, Indiana, which, when fully operational, had the capability of producing up to 1 million biological bombs per month. After the war, the Vigo plant was converted to produce medicines. But U.S. biological weapons research continued, with secret labs testing biological agents on the unsuspecting populations of some American cities. In 1966, for instance, a biological agent called *Bacillus subtilis* was released in New York City's subway system. The test's results showed that releasing an agent in only one subway station could infect the entire underground system, because the trains would push the contaminated air through the tunnels. The total number of people infected in the experiment is unknown.

The British also developed their own biological weapons program that experimented with anthrax and a number of other biological agents. As is true of the Soviet and American programs, the knowledge accumulated by the British in this area still exists in classified documents, and these documents remain a potential threat to the world because of the possibility that they might fall into the wrong hands.

The British, like the Soviets, demonstrated that the other major potential bioweapons threat—namely the possibility of accidents or unintended results—is very real. In 1942, for example, British researchers exploded a bomb laden with anthrax spores near a herd of sheep on the Scottish island of Gruinard. Afterward, they buried the sheep by using a conventional bomb to start a landslide. But the blast blew one of the infected corpses into the sea and it floated to the coast of mainland Scotland, where many local animals contracted anthrax. Later, a Scandinavian couple accidentally landed on the island after misreading their sailing charts and they, along with their dog, contracted anthrax and died. Even today, many people in the region still call Gruinard "Anthrax Island" and refuse to set foot on it.

Passengers ride the New York City subway in the 1960s. In 1966 a secret U.S. lab tested a biological agent on the city's subway system.

U.S. Officials Contemplate Using Bioweapons

During World War II, the United States had its own secret biological warfare program. And at one point, American military leaders came close to launching biological weapons against the nation's enemies.

[After a serious U.S. defeat in North Africa] in February 1943, [American scientific adviser Stanley P.] Lovell, together with scientists of the Canadian bacteriological warfare program, came up with a scheme in which mixtures including grains attractive to houseflies would be molded into the shape of goat dung, infected with psittacosis and tularemia bacteria, and dropped from planes [into enemy territory]. The resultant preoccupation with disease was intended to draw attention away from interference with the U.S. war effort. [However,] before the military command had to make a decision on [the plan] . . . [the Germans were] in retreat and the plan was dropped.

Quoted in Stephen Endicott and Edward Hagerman, *The United States and Biological Warfare*. Bloomington: University of Indiana Press, 1998, pp. 34–35.

Attempts to Ban State-Sponsored Bioweapons

Experts in biological warfare point out that a majority of people in Britain and other countries are under the impression that such accidents are no longer possible because state-sponsored bioweapons programs have been banned by international law. But this assumption is only partly true. On the one hand, international conventions against the development of biological warfare programs were enacted in the twentieth century. On the other, not all nations signed these conventions. Moreover, some experts assert that even some of those who did sign have continued to conduct experiments in secret, thereby violating the conventions.

These anti–biological warfare conventions have both strengths and weaknesses as international safeguards. The first major convention of this type was the so-called Geneva Protocol, enacted in 1925. The full name of the treaty was the Geneva Protocol for the Prohibition of the Use in War of Asphyxiating, Poisonous, or Other Gases and Bacteriological Methods of Warfare. The term *bacteriological methods* was the then-current term for what are now called *biological weapons*. Several nations immediately signed the Geneva Protocol. However, a number of others did not—among them the United States. The reason was that U.S. leaders did not want to risk worldwide condemnation if and when they felt they needed to use such weapons against enemies of the United States. It was not until 1974 that the United States finally ratified the protocol.

Biological Warfare Convention

In the long run, the Geneva Protocol failed to stop the proliferation of biological agents and weapons, partly because its wording was sketchy and its bans limited. The document prohibited only the *use* of such bioweapons, for instance. The protocol did not forbid continued research and development, nor did it provide for international inspections of facilities suspected of breaking the treaty.

By the 1960s and 1970s, scientists, political leaders, and concerned public groups around the world saw the need for a new international convention that would supplement and strengthen the Geneva Protocol. In addition, a few national leaders were for the first time willing to call for the elimination of their own biological programs and stockpiles. In 1969, for example, President Richard Nixon ordered that all U.S. biological weapons be destroyed. This dramatic and unprecedented move had the effect of setting the proper climate for the creation of the new international protocol. On April 10, 1972, the United States, the Soviet Union, and eighty-five other countries signed the Biological Warfare Convention (BWC). This agreement, which was ratified by the United Nations, bans the use of biological weapons. It states explicitly:

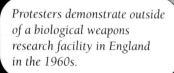

NO
GERM
WARFARE

COMMITTEE OF 100 · SALISBURY JUNE 29
TO VISIT PORTON GERM WARFARE STATION

AGAINST
HE GERMS
OF WAR

NO
GERM
WARFARE

PORTO
GERM WA

WICK
WAST
BRAIN

Protesters demonstrate outside of a biological weapons research facility in England in the 1960s.

> Each State Party to this Convention undertakes never in any circumstances to develop, produce, stockpile or otherwise acquire or retain: (1) Microbial or other biological agents, or toxins whatever their origin or method of production, of types and in quantities that have no justification for . . . protective or other peaceful purposes; (2) Weapons, equipment, or means of delivery designed to use such agents or toxins for hostile purposes or in armed conflict.

This part of the BWC prohibits only the making of biological weapons. Another section of the agreement addresses the problem of eradicating existing stockpiles of weapons:

> Each State Party to this Convention undertakes to destroy, or to divert to peaceful purposes, as soon as possible . . . all agents, toxins, weapons, equipment, and means of delivery . . . which are in its possession or under its jurisdiction or control. In implementing the provisions of this article all necessary safety precautions shall be observed to protect populations and the environment.[12]

The Problem of Russia

The natural question is whether or not the countries that signed the BWC have complied with these provisions. The answer in at least some cases is no. The United States and other nations suspected that the Soviet Union was continuing its bioweapons programs in violation of the BWC. This was proven true when it was discovered that after signing the BWC the Soviets had kept in operation six research facilities and five weapons production plants employing a total of at least fifty-five thousand people. The accident involving the release of anthrax spores at Sverdlovsk in 1979 also showed that the Soviet Union had kept its weaponized anthrax stockpiles in violation of the treaty.

International journalists later discovered and revealed that the Soviets broke their word largely due to lack of trust. Soviet leaders simply did not believe that the Americans had actually destroyed their own biological stockpiles in the 1960s and 1970s. "The thinking inside the Soviet Union," Croddy explains, was that with the United States continuing its offensive research [into biological weapons], the USSR had no choice but to continue as well. And proceed they did. The microbes considered most suitable for weaponization included smallpox virus, anthrax, and plague bacteria. But the Soviet military planners and scientists also studied some 50 other biological agents. Most startling . . . [was] the immense scale of the smallpox program, and the fact that tons of smallpox agent were weaponized for delivery in intercontinental ballistic missiles.[13]

There was a definite change of policy, however, following the collapse of the Soviet Union in the early 1990s. In 1992 the leaders of the now-sovereign state of Russia decided it was time to comply with the provisions of the BWC, and they shut down some of the offending biological weapons facilities. However, others remain operational today. And because these facilities are off-limits to outsiders, it is unclear whether they are in compliance with the treaty. The Russians claim that the buildings are used only to store old supplies of germ cultures, not to make new ones. But as a number of Western experts point out, the very fact that these supplies have not been destroyed is itself probably a violation of the BWC.

Some Western observers are also suspicious that an undetermined amount of research into the development of new bioweapons may still be taking place in secret Russian labs. There, they worry, the same talented scientists who have recently made advances in medicine to cure sick people could be working on biological means to kill other people. The world of secret biological research, investigative journalist Wendy Orent points out,

> is a twisted universe where the man who dreamed of smallpox eradication could design a program that, ultimately, produced weaponized anthrax by the ton. The well-known [Soviet scientist and] defector Kenneth Alibeck . . . described Russia as "a huge country of liars."[14]

Indeed, Alibeck has stated publicly, "What we need to remember is that Russia is a different country [than the United States and other Western nations], with a different mentality. [In Russia] the same person was quite capable of doing humanitarian and immoral work."[15]

The truth of Alibeck's statement seems to have been borne out by a revelation that came to light in 1997 when two Russian scientists admitted to creating a dangerous new potential bioweapon for the Russian military. They transferred genes from a normally harmless bacterium into anthrax spores, resulting in an agent that can destroy human red blood cells. Disturbingly, the existing anthrax vaccines available in the United States are not effective against such a genetically tailored bug.

A storage facility in Russia houses row after row of huge containers holding chemical weapons.

The Danger Posed by Rogue States

The two Russian scientists in question later cooperated with Western scientists and revealed how they made their new anthrax agent. But both biological warfare experts and public officials in many countries are worried that some of the scientists who once worked in the Soviet germ warfare program might become instrumental in the creation of similar programs in other countries. Because the Russians closed down several of their biological warfare facilities, many scientists lost their jobs. Western observers say that some of these individuals have fallen on hard times economically and might be persuaded to sell their weapons-making knowledge to rogue nations such as Iran or North Korea, or even to terrorist groups. In 1995, for instance, some Western journalists reported that recent advances in biological weapons research in Iran may well have been spurred by information provided by former Russian scientists. This could be a serious problem in the future, partly because Iran is only one of several rogue nations that are actively seeking to acquire effective weapons of mass destruction.

Secret Research

The U.S. Central Intelligence Agency (CIA) is conducting a secret program of biodefense research that, in the opinion of many experts, violates the Biological and Toxin Weapons Convention.

Edward Hammond, "Averting Bioterrorism Begins with U.S. Reforms," *Synthesis/Regeneration* 27 (Winter 2002).

One rogue state that the international community long worried about in this regard was Iraq, until 2003 ruled by the brutal dictator Saddam Hussein. It had long been suspected that Iraq had been doing research into biological warfare. That nation signed the BWC in 1972, but Saddam's government officially ratified the treaty only when it was forced to do so after Iraq's defeat in the Gulf War of 1991. Following that conflict, United Nations weapons inspectors entered Iraq and revealed at least some of the extent of the Iraqi bioweapons program. In large

Materials used to create biological weapons are destroyed in Iraq in the 1990s.

part the program operated under the direction of Dr. Rihab Rashid Taha, nicknamed "Doctor Germ" by Western observers. Captured during the U.S. invasion of Iraq in 2003, Taha admitted to making some 5,000 gallons (19,000 l) of botulinum toxin; 2,100 gallons (8,000 l) of anthrax spores; 530 gallons (2,000 l) of cancer-causing toxins; and considerable quantities of camel pox, a disease similar in many respects to smallpox. According to Taha and some other former Iraqi scientists and officials, most or all of these stockpiles were destroyed before 2003. This may be true, as in the wake of the U.S. invasion inspectors were unable find them. Taha herself was later released by the Americans, supposedly in exchange for her cooperation.

Although Iraq is, at least at present, no longer a biological threat to the world community, another rogue state, North Korea, greatly worries many American and other Western observers. In 1996, a high-ranking U.S. government official stated:

> North Korea has pursued research and development related to biological warfare capabilities for the past 30 years. North Korean resources, including a biotechnical infrastructure [i.e., active scientists and labs], are sufficient to support production of limited quantities of infectious biological warfare agents, toxins, and possibly crude biological weapons. North Korea has a wide variety of means available for military delivery of biological warfare agents.[16]

Because North Korea is a closed society with a secretive government, little is known for sure about its biological weapons pro-

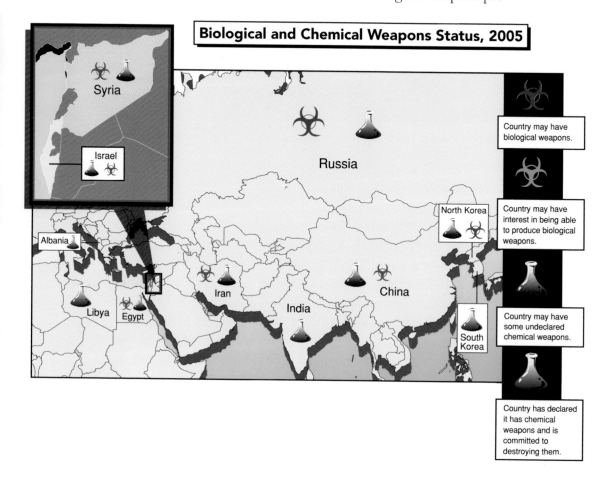

Biological and Chemical Weapons Status, 2005

Syria

Israel

Russia

Albania

North Korea

Iran

China

Libya   Egypt

India

South Korea

Country may have biological weapons.

Country may have interest in being able to produce biological weapons.

Country may have some undeclared chemical weapons.

Country has declared it has chemical weapons and is committed to destroying them.

gram. But some information supplied by defectors suggests that the program is proceeding at full speed. And it is probable that the country has managed to improve on the "crude" bioweapons it possessed back in 1996. The defectors say that North Korean labs have worked on or are presently working with at least thirteen biological agents. Among these are cholera, anthrax, smallpox, bubonic plague, yellow fever, botulinum toxin, and hemorrhagic fever. The South Koreans, who have long feared an attack by the hostile North Koreans, report that half of North Korea's long-range missiles are capable of carrying biological materials, and at least 30 percent of North Korea's large artillery guns, capable of shelling the South Korean capital, have that same capability.

Fear of International Retribution

Other rogue states suspected of having biowarfare programs are Syria and Iran. Yet in addition to the threats posed by rogue states with biological weapons programs, a long list of ordinary nations are suspected of at least maintaining stockpiles of bioweapons. Among others, these states include China, South Africa, Israel, and Egypt.

With so many state-sponsored biological programs and/or stockpiles in the world, some experts say that the likelihood that one of these nations will use these weapons is higher than ever. In contrast, other experts say that the prospects of state-sponsored biological attacks are now low because of fear of retaliation. Biowarfare experts Tara O'Toole and Donald Henderson suggest that "overt use of a biological weapon by a nation-state is unlikely if for no other reason than fear of severe retribution [by other nations] if its role were to be identified."[17] At the same time, however, O'Toole and other experts warn that private extremist and terrorist groups that are not officially connected to an established nation are much less likely to be deterred by fears of retaliation. Thus, the first large-scale biological attack of the twenty-first century, if it does occur, may well be carried out by terrorists.

THE INCREASING AND DAUNTING THREAT OF BIOTERRORISM

In recent years the long-standing threat of biological weapons developed and delivered by sovereign nations, including rogue nations such as Iran and North Korea, has been augmented by a rapidly growing threat from terrorists wielding such weapons. According to experts on terrorism, in most cases terrorists are nonstate actors. This means that they and the groups they belong to, if they are not acting alone, do not work for or represent any particular country. In fact, they may not even share the political ideology of their native land. A clear example is the notorious international criminal Osama bin Laden, whose organization al Qaeda was behind the 9/11 attacks in the United States in 2001. Although he was born in Saudi Arabia, Bin Laden hates the present Saudi regime and has launched attacks on Saudi Arabia as well as on Western countries.

In addition to the United States, Spain and Britain are among the Western countries attacked by al Qaeda and other terrorist groups in recent years. So far, most of the attacks have used conventional weapons, mainly bombs. But some small-scale biological attacks have also been launched by terrorists in the United States and elsewhere. And experts, government officials, and ordinary citizens alike worry that there will be more such attacks in the future. In fact, people everywhere, whether they live in Western or Eastern cultures, want to ensure that these terrible germ weapons are never used again, especially on a large scale.

However, with terrorist groups flourishing more than ever before, this effort is bound to be daunting. And the experts warn that biotterrorism will likely be one of the largest challenges faced by human civilization in the twenty-first century. Frank J. Cilluffo, an American expert on homeland security issues, summarizes the dire dangers and serious challenges that a successful biological attack would pose to the United States as well as other Western countries:

> A successful biological warfare attack on the United States could be a transforming event. Beyond the physical damage and the loss of life, a major biological warfare attack could shake the confidence of our citizens in our government to the core. It potentially threatens our American way of life, tearing at the very fabric of our society. We must grapple with difficult issues such as whether we are protecting America or Americans. Ideally we are defending

Osama bin Laden (center) led the September 11, 2001, attacks on the United States. There is concern that he and other terrorists will turn to biological weapons for other assaults.

both, but no matter how robust our defenses, we will never be able to protect everything, everywhere, all the time, from every potential adversary.[18]

No Longer a Question of If, but of When

The grim scenario Cilluffo describes is based on the assumption that a terrorist group could actually launch a biological attack on the United States or another Western country. Not all that many years ago, such an event would have seemed far-fetched by the vast majority of Americans, something that could happen only in a movie. However, in the last few decades such biological attacks have actually occurred, and the many Americans and other Westerners who rarely read newspapers or watch television newscasts remain unaware of them.

In 1974, for example, forty-eight Italians were arrested on charges that they had poured cultures of cholera germs into Italian public water sources. Six years later, French police found evidence that a German terrorist group called the Red Army Faction was developing biological weapons, including botulinum toxin, in a bathtub in a French apartment. These activities did not result in any injuries or deaths. But in 1984 a terrorist group caused large numbers of people to become gravely ill. Known as the Rashneeshees, this extremist group launched its attack in Wasco County, east of Portland, Oregon, by slipping cultures of salmonella, a microbe that causes severe food poisoning, into salad bars in ten restaurants. Authorities counted 751 cases of the illness; fortunately, no one died in this incident.

Perhaps because there were no fatalities in the Rashneeshee attack, the story more or less came and went in the media. And most of those Americans who did hear about it seem to have considered it a fluke, a bizarre act perpetrated by fanatics and unlikely to be repeated. But only six years later, in March 1990, a Japanese terrorist group called Aum Shinrikyo showed that the Rashneeshee incident was no fluke and that bioterrorism was clearly on the rise. Actually inspired by the Rashneeshees, members of Aum Shinrikyo created masses of botulinum toxin in a secret makeshift lab. Luckily for the intended targets of the 1990 attack, the terrorists lacked the techni-

Members of the Aum Shinrikyo cult march in masks in the likeness of their leader. In 1990 some members of the group attacked a U.S. naval base in Japan with botulinum toxin.

cal knowledge to properly weaponize their deadly cultures, so when they sprayed the toxin into the air at U.S. naval bases in Japan, the poison was not concentrated enough to kill anyone. Members of Aum Shinrikyo also attempted to culture anthrax bacteria and stole Ebola viruses from an African lab. If they had not been caught, they would probably have used these germs in later attacks.

Much more successful than these early, awkward attempts at bioterrorism was the anthrax attack that created death, havoc, and fear in the United States in October and November 2001. Letters containing deadly anthrax spores were delivered to the *New York Post*, NBC anchorman Tom Brokaw, and U.S. senators Tom Daschle and Patrick Leahy. None of these people were infected, but twenty-three other people contracted anthrax, five of whom died from the disease. Most of the victims apparently came into contact with the spores through cross-contamination,

Letter to Senator Daschle

In 2001 Senator Tom Daschle received a letter (above) containing anthrax. He was not harmed, but the attack spread fear across the United States.

when some of the tiny particles leaked from the four envelopes while they were en route to their destinations.

Although the death toll of these anthrax attacks was relatively low, the assaults were highly successful because they fulfilled the main goal of the attacker or attackers—they spread fear through the entire U.S. population. For weeks after the incidents the media reported numerous instances in which quantities of unidentified white, powdery substances were spotted in various towns and cities; local evacuations ensued while teams of investigators wearing special protective suits examined the powders. Most of these events turned out to be false alarms. But they served notice to the Western world that the age of bioterrorism had definitely arrived. Noted biowarfare expert Barry R. Schneider points out:

> This late 2001 series of anthrax attacks via the U.S. Postal Service fulfilled the warnings of those who had warned of

the inevitability of future bio-terrorist events. [These] attacks . . . validated the previous warnings by some experts concerning bio-terrorism that it was not a question of "if," it was a question of "when." Now such bio-terrorism is a historical fact, not just a prediction of the future.[19]

Foreign Terrorists and Their Motives

The identities of the terrorists who placed anthrax spores in letters in the United States in 2001 remain unknown. A number of experts think they may well have been foreign-born individuals. In fact, some still suspect al Qaeda, though no definite proof has linked the attacks to that organization. Certainly al Qaeda and other well-known foreign terrorist groups are capable of such mayhem. In fact, members of these groups have publicly warned that they will use any means available to them to cripple America and other Western societies.

In the face of these overt threats, military officials and various experts in the West are diligently trying to find and destroy the bases and operatives of foreign terrorist groups. Just as important in the ongoing "war on terror," as U.S. president George W. Bush described the situation soon after the 9/11 attacks, is trying to identify terrorists who are less well known or still unidentified. To do this, leaders in the war on terror first attempt to profile terrorists; that is, they try to determine what sort of person becomes a terrorist and why he or she chooses to commit such heinous acts.

Such profiles indicate that most terrorists are nonstate actors. In fact, studies by the experts have revealed that nonstate terrorists are, in particular, more likely than established nation-states to commit acts of bioterrorism. This is in large part because it is more difficult for the victim of such an attack to retaliate against a nonstate person or group. As Cilluffo explains:

> Unlike their state-sponsored counterparts, non-state actors are much freer from the constraints of retaliation, making them more likely to use biological agents. After all, it is hard to retaliate against an actor if there is no return address.[20]

Assassination by a Biological Agent

In at least one case in recent times, a biological attack has been aimed at an individual person rather than the general population, as recounted here by healthcare expert Thomas J. Johnson. The biological agent used was the toxin ricin.

Georgi Markov died after someone punctured his leg with a ricin capsule.

On September 7, 1978, Georgi Markov, a Bulgarian writer and journalist . . . left home for work. . . . As Markov neared the queue [line] of people waiting for the bus, he suddenly felt a stinging pain in the back of his right thigh. He turned and saw a heavyset man . . . stooping over to pick up a dropped umbrella. The man hailed a taxi and disappeared. Unconcerned, Markov continued to work, where he told his colleagues what happened. He showed one BBC friend a red pimple-like swelling on his thigh. That evening Markov developed a high fever and he was taken to a London hospital and treated for a nonspecific type of blood poisoning. Three days later he was dead. On autopsy a tiny pellet was found in the wound in Markov's thigh. . . . Toxicology results determined that Markov had been murdered by a poison, ricin. The ricin was encapsulated in a waxy base designed to melt at body temperature thus releasing [the poison] into the tissues.

Thomas J. Johnson, "A History of Biological Warfare from 300 B.C. to the Present," American Association for Respiratory Care. www.aarc.org/resources/biologicial/history.asp.

The low risk of capture and punishment is not the only reason that an increasing number of foreign terrorists are considering or planning to use biological weapons. Indeed, bioweapons are emerging as weapons of choice also because they are relatively inexpensive and easy to produce. "With a few thousand dollars," Davis says, "one would have sufficient funds to acquire, produce, and deploy bacterial agents that could kill thousands of people."[21] Moreover, most deadly germs and toxins are fairly easy to administer in aerosols, which can spread them throughout a crowded area, such as a subway station, airport terminal, or skyscraper. Thus, the exposure of large numbers of victims to a biological agent would be assured.

Furthermore, such an attack would be silent, in contrast to a bomb explosion, and the victims would not know they had been targeted until later, when large numbers of them began to get sick simultaneously. This would give the attackers plenty of time to get away and cover their tracks. Still another advantage of a biological approach for a terrorist is the potential number of casualties that can be inflicted. If a lethal enough agent is used, the attackers have a better chance of creating a large death toll, as well as frightening

Deadly toxins that are distributed with aerosols can spread quickly in crowded areas such as an airport (pictured).

the rest of the population of the targeted city and nation. Finally, in the psyche of a terrorist, a successful biological attack seems to be a way to gain attention and political leverage. Thereafter, the terrorist reasons, he or she "will neither be trifled with nor ignored on the world stage," Croddy suggests. "Once accepted as a player in the [biological weapons] business in a serious way, almost any organization has strategic clout."[22]

The Threat of Domestic Bioterrorism

So far, the main focus of the examination of bioterrorists and their motives has been on foreign individuals and groups. However, experts are quick to point out that the threat of domestic terrorists who might use biological weapons against their own countrymen is no less worrisome. Extremist Timothy McVeigh's successful and devastating demolition of the Murrah Federal Building in Oklahoma City in 1995 shows that foreign nations are not the only ones that have bred terrorists. Though McVeigh used an explosive device, a number of other domestic terrorists, including the Rashneeshees in 1984, have used or have contemplated using biological agents.

Unprecedented Challenges

The threat of bio-terrorism by states and non-state actors presents unprecedented planning challenges to American government and society.

Frank J. Cillufo, testimony before the U.S. Senate Committee on Foreign Relations, September 5, 2001.

In some cases, the motivations of domestic bioterrorists are similar to those of their foreign counterparts. Both might want to call attention to a particular political cause they advocate and fight for, and in the view of a terrorist born and bred in America's democratic society, his or her biological attack might constitute a form of civic protest. This was indeed the motivation of a domestic group calling itself the Patriots Council. In 1994 these so-called patriots planned to protest against what they saw as unfair U.S. tax laws by using deadly ricin toxin to kill several U.S. agents. The culprits were captured, however, before they could put their plan into action.

The ruins of the federal building in Oklahoma City, bombed by Timothy McVeigh in 1995, are a reminder of the threat of domestic terrorism.

Other common motives of domestic bioterrorists are best described as religious or racist. The two are often linked, because many who claim they possess racial superiority believe their ideology is ordained and sanctioned by God. Typically, these individuals and groups view existing laws and leaders as illegitimate. Thus, "they are unconstrained by fear of government or public backlash," Harvard University scholar and terrorism expert Jessica Stern points out.

> Their actions are carried out to please God and themselves, not to impress [everyday citizens]. Frequently, they do not claim credit for their attacks, since their ultimate objective is to create so much fear and chaos that the government's legitimacy is destroyed. Their victims are often viewed as subhuman since they are outside the group's religion or race.[23]

Such feelings of racial and religious superiority were behind a planned domestic bio-attack in 1972. Members of an extreme right-wing group called the Rising Sun, who wanted to promote a white master race, were arrested in Chicago in the nick of time. They were in possession of several pounds of typhoid fever cultures with which they were going to poison the city's water supply. Three years later, members of an extreme left-wing group, the Symbionese Liberation Army, were caught with technical manuals on how to manufacture bioweapons.

Still another potential cause of domestic biological terrorist attacks is what experts call the copycat phenomenon. In such cases, would-be terrorists are inspired by and want to imitate antisocial and criminal acts perpetrated by other terrorists. A

Larry Wayne Harris (left) is escorted by a police officer after his arrest for possessing bubonic plague and anthrax bacteria. Harris had planned to assassinate President Bill Clinton in the 1990s.

well-documented example occurred in the 1990s. In 1995 Larry Wayne Harris, leader of an extremist group called the Republic of Texas, was greatly impressed with the sarin gas attack launched that year in the subways of Tokyo, Japan, by members of Aum Shinrikyo. Harris wanted to assassinate President Bill Clinton. To this end, he acquired three vials containing bubonic plague bacteria and some considerable quantities of anthrax bacteria. The authorities apprehended him in 1998 before he could use these deadly agents, but for nearly a year after news of his aborted attack was released, other copycats imitated Harris by issuing threats to launch their own anthrax attacks or staging hoaxes designed to make it look as if they had done so.

Although the exact motives of domestic bioterrorists vary, experts recognize one important factor that all of them have in common. Both individual terrorists and the leaders and followers of terrorist groups are attracted to violence for its own sake. They then try to rationalize their fascination with violence by saying that violent acts are the only way to achieve their stated political, religious, or racist goals. "Groups may also become most violent," Stern adds, "when the state is closing in on them, potentially posing difficulties for those fighting terrorism."[24]

Targeting a U.S. City

Whether today's potential bioterrorists are foreign-born or domestic, in theory no nation is safe from them. However, experts recognize that the number-one target of such disgruntled people is the United States, either the nation itself or its military forces and/or diplomatic representatives around the world. The motives for singling out the United States vary but fall into a few general categories. The first is dissatisfaction with the U.S. role as the sole superpower on the globe. Terrorists who think this way would like to reduce U.S. influence and power. Second, some bioterrorists see the United States, the world's wealthiest nation, as too dominant an economic competitor and hope to level the international financial playing field. Still other motivations for attacking the United States are religious differences, hate, and revenge for supposed wrongs committed by the U.S. government against other countries.

Whatever reason an individual or group might have for unleashing biological weapons on the United States or its forces, experts say that a few possible scenarios are the most likely ones to occur, and therefore public officials, especially those working for the Homeland Security Department, should concentrate most of their time and energy preparing for these. The first is a biological attack on a U.S. population center. In fact, the experts point out, the most effective strategy for the terrorists would be to try to attack two or more cities simultaneously because it would maximize both the number of deaths and the spread of fear among the rest of the population. Indeed, this was a fundamental aspect of the 9/11 attack plan, which targeted both New York and Washington, D.C. Originally, still other U.S. cities were intended targets, but the attackers decided that moving against more than two would be too logistically difficult at the time.

No matter how many U.S. cities may be targeted by the terrorists, experts say that the most likely weapon of choice will be anthrax spores. First, the disease is not contagious, but rather is usually contracted only from direct exposure to the spores. Therefore, the attackers would not need to worry that they would carry the disease back to their homeland or headquarters. Also, the symptoms of anthrax take a while to appear, so the terrorists would be able to release the spores and then leave the United States before anyone even knew an attack had occurred. Finally, the amount of spores needed to attack a city is relatively low. A bag weighing less than a hundred pounds would be sufficient, and its contents could be dispersed quite easily from a moving plane, boat, or car.

Other Possible Bioterrorist Scenarios

Another kind of bioterrorist threat against the United States that experts say is likely in the future is an agroterrorist attack. As Anne Kohnen, of the Belfer Center for Science and International Affairs, warns:

> Agricultural targets are "soft targets," or ones that maintain such a low level of security that a terrorist could carry out an attack unobserved. Biological agents are

small, inexpensive, and nearly impossible to detect. A terrorist may choose to use biological weapons against agriculture simply because it is the easiest and cheapest way to cause large-scale damage.[25]

Kohnen and other experts point out that besides being easy and cheap, agroterrorism may be attractive for those few terrorists who retain some moral constraints. In other words, a recruit who is reluctant to commit mass murder might have few or no moral qualms about inflicting economic damage on the United States by destroying crops and livestock. Another advantage for the attackers would be anonymity. Experts acknowledge that unless the agroterrorists were unduly inept and sloppy in their efforts, finding them would be nearly impossible.

Chicken is dumped in Belgium because of fears that it may be contaminated with dioxin. Poisoning livestock to make it unavailable for sale is an example of agroterrorism.

There is no doubt that a successful agroterrorist attack against the United States could be potentially devastating. In the late 1990s, Belgium suffered a terrorist assault in which someone placed dioxin, a harmful chemical, in local chicken feed. That nation's economy suffered an estimated $1 billion in losses as a result. A single agroterrorist attack in the United States, some experts estimate, could cost the country $100 billion or more, not to mention the fear and social disruptions it would cause.

A third likely scenario for bioterrorist attacks against the United States would be an attack on U.S. forces stationed in the Middle East. The goal would be to force the United States to withdraw its troops from that region. One approach would be to sneak some sort of biological agent onto a U.S. base in Iraq or Kuwait and unleash the germs or toxins. Even if only ten or twenty U.S. soldiers died of anthrax or some other deadly agent, experts say, fear would spread through both U.S. forces and the population back in the United States. If more such at-

A Narrow Escape from Death by Anthrax

The threat of bioterrorists attacking U.S. troops in the Middle East is much more real than many people imagine. In fact, evidence discovered later showed that the American soldiers who liberated Kuwait from Iraq in the 1991 Gulf War narrowly escaped a large-scale biological attack. Iraq's dictator, Saddam Hussein, had earlier ordered the development of anthrax spores weaponized in the form of aerosol sprays. In addition, Saddam had a jet aircraft equipped with heavy-duty spray equipment and hid the plane only a few miles from the main path of U.S. forces. At the order of the Iraq tyrant, the plane would have dispensed the lethal spores onto the Americans, which would have killed an estimated seventy thousand or more of them. In the end, Saddam refrained from using the anthrax because he feared the United States would retaliate with nuclear weapons.

tacks occurred, it is possible that worried U.S. officials might begin troop withdrawals—or at least that is what the terrorists hope would happen. Another approach would be to unleash the biological agents on the locals and then publicly accuse U.S. troops of using their own biological weapons; in this way, the terrorists could attempt to discredit the United States in the eyes of people across the globe.

Perception Versus Reality

Biological weapons are widely viewed with dread, though in actual use they have rarely done great harm.

Gregg Easterbrook. "The Meaninglessness of Term Limits," *New Republic*, October 7, 2002.

These examples make it clear that would-be bioterrorists have many potential avenues of attack against the United States and other countries. And no nation or government can afford to make the mistake of not taking such threats seriously. "Bio-terrorist threats are real," Davis says, "and require the full commitment of the United States and its allies to have a well-funded biodefense effort."[26]

BUILDING UP DEFENSES AGAINST BIOLOGICAL ATTACKS

Although neither the idea nor the practice of biological warfare is new, the threat of biological attacks against individuals, cities, and nations is now greater than ever. The anthrax scare that occurred in the United States shortly after the 9/11 attacks in 2001 made this clear by raising public awareness of the problem. People of all walks of life learned that a few terrorists and other individuals are more than willing to commit mass murder using germs and/or deadly toxins. There was also heightened public awareness that a number of rogue nations might have stockpiles of bioweapons and under certain circumstances might well use them against other countries.

In view of these emerging and in many ways scary realities, since 2001 concerned people across the globe have increasingly considered what they can do to defend themselves, their families, and their communities from biological attacks. As a result, some defensive measures against biological weapons are now in place in various countries, including the United States. These include emergency plans to handle sudden outbreaks of disease; stepped-up security in office buildings, sports stadiums, and other places where large numbers of people gather; drills staged periodically to prepare first responders such as police, firefighters, contagious disease experts, and medical personnel for emergencies; expansion of the resources of public health departments to make them better able to respond to a biological attack; the manufacture of large quantities of existing vaccines that might need to be administered to millions of citizens following a major biological attack; and other related measures.

Some progress has definitely been made in each of these areas since 2001 in the United States and other industrialized nations. However, few involved in these efforts feel that existing defenses against the threat of biological weapons are yet fully adequate. Such misgivings are strongly echoed by the experts on the subject, who point out that more money needs to be spent on improving the existing defenses. Most countries "have a long way to go," Schneider asserts,

> to catch up to the biological weapons threats that have emerged at the beginning of the twenty-first century. . . . The United States and its allies are far behind the threat posed by bio-terrorists and [national] adversaries willing

U.S. Marines practice a response to biological terrorism. Some experts feel that most countries are underprepared for such attacks.

to use bio-warfare. . . . Hopefully . . . U.S. and allied officials [will] do much more. Needed is investment in vaccines and other biodefense programs to close the threat/response gap that has widened through years of looking the other way and failing to recognize the great menace that biological warfare and bio-terrorism pose.[27]

Thus, building up defenses against potential biological attacks must be an ongoing effort. Although strides have been made in recent years, there are still some areas in which improvement is needed.

Government Emergency Plans and Trained Responders

Government leaders and agencies stand at the forefront of the efforts to build up both national and local defenses against biological weapons. It is the responsibility of these leaders and agencies to make public policy related to the problem, for example. More specifically, government entities are charged with putting emergency plans into place. One important aspect of such plans, of course, is notifying first responders and the public of the emergency. A number of warning systems, old and new, exist for this purpose. Among them are the National Warning System (NAWAS) and Emergency Broadcast System (EBS).

Government officials acknowledge that warnings are merely a first step. Once notified of the emergency, trained first responders must speed into action and follow plans designed to contain or neutralize the threat. Experts say that some of the existing anti–biological warfare plans in the United States are well thought out and comprehensive and may work well in an emergency. One often-touted example is the range of federal, state, and local response plans for a possible agroterrorist attack using foot-and-mouth disease or some other dangerous agent. In the event of such an attack, local farmers and animal handlers, including veterinarians, would constitute the first line of defense. Because they deal with the nation's livestock daily, they are in the best position to recognize when something unusual is happening, particularly the appearance of a so-called foreign animal disease (FAD).

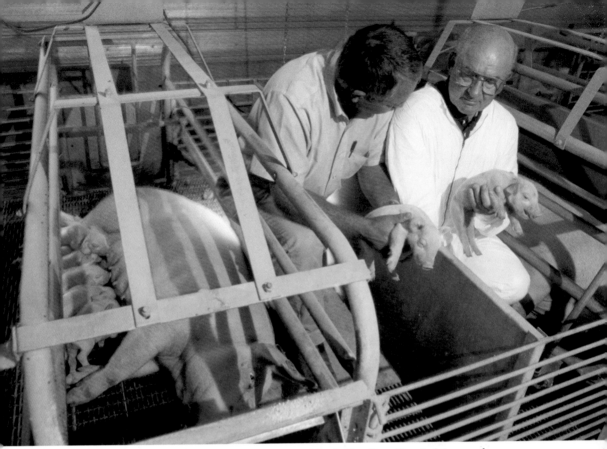

A veterinarian (right) examines a pig in North Carolina. Veterinarians and farmers are the first line of defense against agroterrorism because they would immediately notice problems with livestock.

If the locals are convinced that the threat of a FAD is real, the plan calls for them to alert the Animal and Plant Health Inspection Service (APHIS), a special unit of the U.S. Department of Agriculture. Peterson describes APHIS as:

> the lead agency responsible for the diagnosis and management of all suspicious agricultural disease outbreaks. It has a memorandum of understanding with every state and the Department of Defense to cooperate in disease emergencies, and it has the authority to seize property and eliminate all animal hosts within certain . . . quarantine zones. In the event of a foot-and-mouth disease agro-terrorist attack, the APHIS division would coordinate the entire emergency response plan with state veterinary officials, veterinary colleges, industry officials,

the Department of Defense, the Federal Emergency Management Agency (FEMA) . . . private veterinarians, and livestock producers.[28]

During such an emergency APHIS officials would assign specially trained agents called foreign animal disease diagnosticians, or FADDs, to investigate, draw conclusions, and report back. Presently, the United States has about 350 FADDs scattered across the country.

If APHIS officials feel that the outbreak of FMD or some other disease caused by the attackers is too big for them to handle alone, they are ready to call on another organization for help. This is the Regional Emergency Animal Disease Eradica-

Government officials in Argentina inspect a cow for foot-and-mouth disease. In the United States, several government organizations work together to contain animal diseases.

tion Organization, or READEO. Two thirty-eight-member READEO teams exist in the United States today, one stationed in the eastern part of the nation, the other in the west. These individuals are a mix of veterinarians, animal and plant experts, experts from the U.S. Department of Agriculture, and military support personnel.

Experts say that the APHIS and READEO systems are well organized and the teams well trained. And as long as a potential biological attack is fairly small in scope, members of these teams will likely do an excellent job of quickly containing the threat. Yet budgetary problems have brought about an ominous reduction in the number of these first responders in recent years. Six READEO teams existed in the 1980s; that number was reduced to four in the 1990s and to two in recent years. "Clearly this trend must stop," Peterson contends. "While most experts agree that the current APHIS/READEO system could respond adequately to a single point agro-terrorist attack, a large-scale or multiple point attack would overwhelm the current system."[29]

Drills to Test and Improve Response Capabilities

Systems similar to APHIS and READEO are now in place in the United States to deal with biological attacks against human populations. Local law enforcement officers, firefighters, public officials, and medical personnel constitute the first line of defense because they are the ones who will likely recognize the outbreak of disease or mass poisoning if and when it occurs. These individuals will also be among the initial first responders. They will secure various public buildings and sites in hopes of containing the outbreak, call in trained medical and military teams if necessary to help any victims, and begin identifying and apprehending the attackers.

Since the 9/11 attacks, the U.S. government has allocated extra funds to these first responders. Much of the money has been spent on stockpiling emergency clothing, including bio-hazard suits designed to keep germs out. Many local first response units have also bought better germ detection equipment

Avoid Public Distrust and Anger?

Since the 9/11 attacks in 2001, a number of states in the United States have proposed changing health laws and other laws to give state officials more power to prevent biological and other attacks. Here Twila Brase, president of the Citizen's Council on Health Care in St. Paul, Minnesota, argues that giving state governments too much power might threaten civil liberties and make the citizens angry.

Public trust requires thoughtful contingency plans that uphold constitutional rights and freedom of conscience, support medical ethics, and encourage voluntary cooperation with disease containment strategies. State legislatures should not rush to enact ill-conceived, ineffective legislation. Public policy must always recognize and respect the rights, dignity, and intelligence of individuals. An angry public is not a cooperative public. If health officials are empowered to harm the very people legislators want to protect, a public health emergency may soon become a crisis of the public's trust.

Twila Brase, "A Model for Medical Tyranny," *Ideas on Liberty*, August 2002, p. 11.

and first-aid supplies. However, there is a general consensus among local officials that many such units are not yet satisfactorily prepared and could use still more federal and state monies.

Some of the existing monies allocated for biodefense in the United States have been and continue to be used for live drills. In these exercises, local first responders stage mock biological attacks in an effort to test and improve their abilities to respond to such emergencies. So far the results of these drills have been very revealing.

For example, in June 2001, large numbers of public officials and first responders around the country took part in a major drill called a bioterrorist attack simulation. It was designed and overseen by four leading biological warfare experts—Tara O'Toole and Thomas Inglesby of the Johns Hopkins Center for Civilian

Biodefense Strategies, and Randy Larsen and Mark DeMier of the organization ANSER (Advancing National Strategies and Enabling Results). Titled Operation Dark Winter the exercise simulated the possible outcomes of a rogue nation releasing smallpox germs in American cities. In the drill, agents from the rogue nation secretly spread the germs in shopping malls, and the disease spread with alarming rapidity. At the end of the first day alone, thirty-four cases of smallpox were detected in Oklahoma, nine in Georgia, and seven in Pennsylvania. By the sixth day, there were two thousand cases of smallpox in fifteen states and hospitals were overwhelmed. Angry mobs began to crowd health clinics, demanding to be vaccinated. At the end of two weeks, a thousand victims were dead, the disease had spread to other countries, and medical officials feared the loss of 3 million lives in the next three months.

Most of the U.S. government officials, politicians, medical personnel, and first responders who took part in this drill were genuinely surprised by its grim outcome. According to one observer:

> Most of them later concluded that the exercise had demonstrated how unprepared the United States was for biological warfare or terrorist acts. Problems ranged from shortages of needed medicines to confusion among local, state, and federal officials over who had authority to deal with the crisis. Dr. Margaret Hamburg, who played the role of the head of the U.S. Department of Health and Human Services in the simulation, said it left the participants humbled by what they did not know and could not do, and convinced of the urgent need to better prepare the nation against this gruesome threat.[30]

O'Toole and other experts at the Johns Hopkins Center were also instrumental in staging a larger-scale biological warfare drill in 2005. Called Atlantic Storm, it placed the president of the United States, played in the exercise by former U.S. secretary of state Madeleine Albright, and eight other world leaders in a summit meeting in Washington, D.C. During the meeting, news came that smallpox germs had been released in several countries by a splinter group of the terrorist organization al Qaeda. These leaders attempted to respond to the crisis. But their countries' resources were ultimately overwhelmed, and at the end of six months the worldwide death toll was in the millions and the global economy had ground nearly to a standstill. Once again, the results of the drill were revealing and disturbing. "It was a shock how little prepared many countries were,"[31] commented the Dutch official who portrayed his country's prime minister in the simulation.

The Role of Doctors and Other Public Health Personnel

Though public officials and planners play a central role in preparing to deal with potential biological crises, diagnosing the initial victims, curing them, and trying to keep the disease from spreading will be the job of doctors, nurses, paramedics, and other trained health personnel. David Stripp, a science writer for *Fortune* magazine, says, "The horrible burden [of being the first line of defense] will fall on hospitals and public health agencies that are hard-pressed even to handle their everyday workloads."[32]

National Security

From a national security perspective, a preemptive but voluntary smallpox vaccination program for the general public in addition to a more comprehensive vaccination of military personnel and first responders makes sense.

Michael Scardaville, "Public Health and National Security Planning: The Case for Voluntary Smallpox Vaccination," *Heritage Foundation Backgrounder*, December 6, 2002.

Indeed, though the vast majority of public health personnel are skilled and dedicated, they themselves recognize that the present resources and training they possess may be inadequate in a real biological warfare emergency. When a group of medical personnel and other first responders attended a seminar in

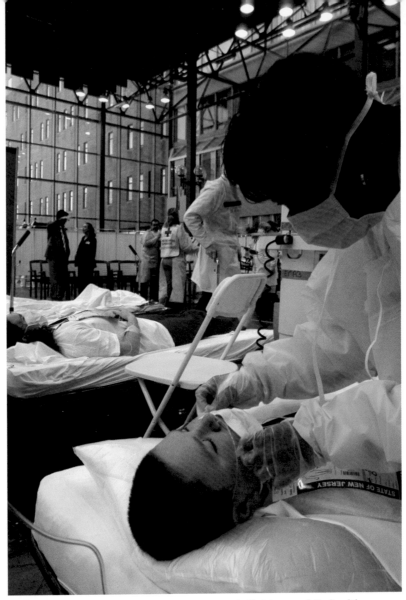

A patient is treated during an antiterrorism drill. Many public health workers are not fully prepared to deal with a biological crisis.

bioterrorism preparedness, they gave themselves an overall rating of only 4.1 out of a possible 10 for their own response capabilities. Many recognized the real possibility that many doctors and nurses would not initially recognize that a disease they were seeing in their emergency rooms had been spread by malicious attackers. Indeed, "it is doubtful that anyone would notice," expert Barbara F. Bullock comments, that the influx of patients currently being treated in multiple emergency facilities came from the same geographical area. The patients would be treated by another set of physicians who are even less likely . . . to recognize the symptoms that manifest from exposure to biological attacks, since few [modern] physicians have seen a case of anthrax, smallpox, or the plague.[33]

It has also been demonstrated that few diagnostic laboratories in the United States possess the resources to rapidly confirm the presence of these otherwise rare diseases. As a result of these deficiencies, Bullock and other experts have called for the installation of improved laboratory instruments and more and

No Need for Mass Smallpox Vaccinations?

Some biological warfare and medical experts think that vaccinating the entire U.S. population against smallpox as a preventive measure is a good idea. But some others disagree, including Robert C. Cihak and Michael A. Glueck of the Association of American Physicians and Surgeons.

While immunizing or protecting everybody against all possible threats might seem like a logical option, in reality it would not be necessary or desirable. America's high standard of living allows a great deal of flexibility in responding to possible emergencies. . . . Because of medical advances in supportive medical treatment and the relatively small supply of vaccine now available, we agree with public health experts who recommend holding off vaccinating the general public . . . until there is a demonstrated outbreak [of smallpox]. . . . so long as threats remain hypothetical, the general public should not be encouraged or required to risk injury or death from treatments they may never need.

Robert C. Cihak and Michael A. Glueck, *Insight on the News*, January 7, 2002.

better training of medical personnel to recognize a biological attack when it occurs. Other suggestions for improvement include developing new, cutting-edge diagnostic tools that could identify the presence of biological agents within thirty minutes, organizing special teams of doctors and nurses who could respond to biological attacks quickly and efficiently, creating new plans to coordinate these responders and other health-care professionals with state and federal public officials, and stockpiling vaccines to safeguard human and animal populations from the spread of diseases caused by biological agents.

Employing Existing and New Vaccines

Vaccines will be among the principal tools used by health-care professionals to combat diseases spread during biological attacks. There is no doubt that vaccines can be effective in preventing or fighting disease epidemics. However, doctors and other experts agree that stockpiles of many needed vaccines are low, and it is very expensive either to make millions of new doses of existing vaccines or to create new ones. Schneider briefly summarizes recent deficiencies in U.S. national vaccine supplies:

> Of the fourteen diseases that experts deem most lethal, effective, and weaponizable, the United States currently has FDA [Food and Drug Administration]–approved vaccines for only four agents (anthrax, smallpox, cholera, and plague). Five are in the investigational new drug category . . . and may be years away from final approval. In the case of [the] five other diseases . . . no vaccines of any kind currently exist.[34]

Clearly, the United States and its allies need to step up their efforts to create vaccines to meet potential bioweapons threats.

Yet developing and stockpiling vaccines represents only part of the challenge in using them in biological warfare emergencies. Another aspect of the issue is that many Americans find mass inoculations with vaccines unacceptable, or at least controversial. The existing vaccine for anthrax is an instructive case in point. It is generally effective, and tens of thousands of U.S.

service personnel have received it thus far. However, it requires six separate inoculations, plus boosters each subsequent year, and it can have some unpleasant side effects. Thus, the vaccine is not "user-friendly," as Croddy puts it,

> and undertaking a program to conduct a blanket vaccination of every man, woman, and child in the country would be fraught with problems. Even if the anthrax vaccine were made available to the public . . . individuals would want to think carefully before going through the time and effort. A nation-wide anthrax vaccination program, albeit unlikely to ever be implemented, deserves a frank and public discussion before it is ever put in place.[35]

Although mass vaccinations for anthrax seem unlikely in the near future, in recent years a number of experts and other concerned individuals have called for administering the smallpox vaccine on a national scale as a preventive measure against a biological attack. University of California historian Louis Warren warns:

> Smallpox can spread before symptoms, which begin with fever and aches, are recognized. Even when the afflicted begin to get sick, few doctors would be able to diagnose this now unfamiliar killer before thousands, perhaps hundreds of thousands, were infected. Should it be sprayed from an aerosol container aboard a plane or two, it could rapidly spread across the country.

Warren and those who agree with him point out that vaccination campaigns have been highly successful in the past against deadly diseases, including measles, mumps, and diphtheria, as well as smallpox itself. "Such campaigns are not nearly as difficult as guarding skyscrapers from hijacked jetliners," he says.

> They are easier and cheaper than patrolling borders, detecting money laundering or finding fugitive terrorists. . . . It may be that spreading smallpox hasn't been easy for terrorists to accomplish. We might even have time to inoculate everybody before they can succeed.[36]

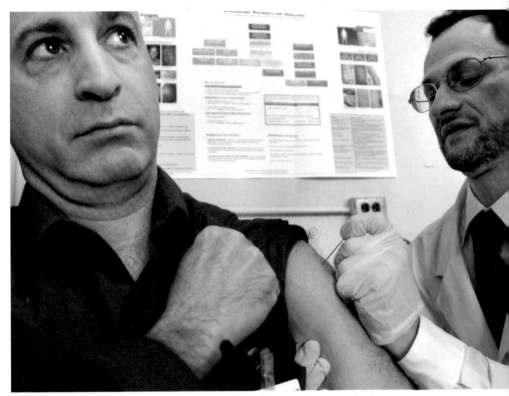

A doctor receives a smallpox vaccination. Public health officials and others disagree on the value of vaccinating all Americans against smallpox.

In contrast, other experts insist that mass smallpox vaccinations before any biological attack had occurred would waste precious resources and unnecessarily scare the citizenry. In addition, critics say, the vaccination programs could also end up killing people. According to Steven Black of the Kaiser Permanente Vaccine Study Center in Oakland, California:

> One out of 500,000 individuals will die as a direct cause of the vaccine. Although the risk of either death or . . . severe side effects may sound relatively rare, vaccination of the entire U.S. population would result in 600 deaths and 2,000 individuals with serious brain infections. These very real risks must be balanced against what is currently only a theoretical risk of smallpox being introduced by terrorists.[37]

A community volunteer discusses tuberculosis prevention with a family in New York in 1908 as part of a public awareness campaign.

Black adds that localized smallpox vaccinations in given regions would be prudent after a confirmed biological attack in those regions. Thus, vaccines may prove to be important tools in biodefense efforts even if mass inoculations on a national scale are never employed.

The Role of Public Health Laws

According to a number of experts and public officials, reforming and streamlining public health laws is another potential tool in biodefense efforts. Yet despite the increasing threat of bioterrorism, the idea of making major changes in U.S. public health laws remains more controversial than most people realize. Some experts point out that these laws are outmoded and need to be changed to make them work better against potential bioterrorists. In fact, according to Lawrence O. Gostin, who teaches public health at Johns Hopkins University, "Public-health laws across the country are highly antiquated, built up in layers during the last century."[38] Shannon Brownlee, a journalist who specializes in health care, agrees, pointing out that few substantive changes have been made in these laws in the past hundred years. "In the late nineteenth and early twentieth centuries," she says,

> each new disease—cholera, polio, syphilis, tuberculosis— triggered new legislation, granting public health officials specific powers to identify and test the sick, quarantine or treat them as necessary, and require the rest of the population to take preventive measures aimed at stopping the spread of infection. This disease-by-disease approach worked well enough, given the times and crudeness of medical care, but it has bequeathed us a confusing patchwork of statutes ill-suited to modern threats.[39]

One clear example Brownlee cites is the case of anthrax. Because the disease does not normally pass from person to person, many state laws covering communicable diseases may not apply to anthrax. This might well hamper state officials, including first responders, in dealing with local outbreaks in a speedy, efficient manner. For example, state officials might not have the legal authority to shut down trains on which they suspect victims of anthrax are riding.

Unsafe Vaccine?

Unfortunately, the smallpox vaccine is just not as safe as any of the other vaccines routinely used in the United States today.

Steven Black, "Smallpox Sense," ABC News, December 24, 2001. www.vaccination news.com/DailyNews/December2001/SmallpoxSense.htm.

However, other experts and concerned citizens see major changes in the nation's health laws as unwise because they might pose a threat to civil liberties. In particular, these individuals worry that changes in the laws will grant too much power to state governors and the leading health officials working under them. In theory, these officials might force many citizens to give up their privacy, or even control over their own bodies, in the name of public safety. Twila Brase, of the Citizens' Council on Health Care in St. Paul, Minnesota, claims that after the 9/11 attacks, some states enacted new health laws that diminished the civil rights of the citizens of those states. She sums up the problem this way:

> [In such cases] a state's governor [would have] sole discretion to declare a public-health emergency. Once the emergency [is] declared, public-health officials would assume police powers, the militia would be mobilized, and the legislature would be prohibited from intervening for 60 days. . . . Existing laws and individual rights could be suspended. . . . Individuals [would be required] to submit to state-ordered vaccinations, examination, testing, treatment, and specimen collection. Resisters would be charged with a misdemeanor and quarantined.[40]

This sharp difference of opinion about changing health-care laws to better deal with the threat of biological attacks, like the issue of mass vaccinations, demonstrates that preparation for and appropriate public responses to such attacks are far from simple and obvious. Indeed, they are complex issues relating to individual privacy, civil liberties, personal and public safety, and the proper role of government in the lives of citizens in an open democracy. Some people advocate doing whatever seems necessary to protect the public from harm, even if some freedoms must be sacrificed. Others disagree and repeat a famous quote attributed to one of America's Founding Fathers, Benjamin Franklin: "They who would give up essential liberty to purchase a little temporary safety, deserve neither liberty or safety."[41] It appears that few, if any, of these contentious issues will be resolved until the United States or another nation faces one or more large-scale biological attacks. Such events, if they ever do happen, will force those in charge to make definite decisions one way or another.

CHAPTER
5

PREVENTING FUTURE BIOLOGICAL WEAPONS THREATS

M any people today are worried about the possible use of biological weapons, either by rogue nations or by terrorists working independently of national entities. A number of experts on the subject say that such fears are not misplaced. In fact, they point out that the already potent threat of biological warfare could actually get worse in the not-too-distant future. This is not only because there are increasing numbers of angry or unstable individuals who might resort to bioterrorism to further their personal aims; another reason the danger will likely increase, experts say, is that the march of technology will likely open up new and deadly means for making and delivering biological agents. Indeed, a study sponsored by the U.S. Department of Defense stated, "There is enormous potential—based on advances in modern molecular biology . . . for making [more] sophisticated [biological] weapons."[42]

Among these advances is the development of so-called binary biological weapons. These weapons can be made by culturing some seemingly harmless microbes and combining them with special DNA fragments. When these fragments are combined with the germs, the latter suddenly become harmful to humans and/or animals. Designer genes, or genes that have been mechanically altered to function in a specific way, also pose an increasing threat. The complete DNA sequences of more than thirty kinds of bacteria and more than six hundred kinds of viruses are already known. Moreover, most of this information has been published on the Internet. As the widely respected military and medical expert

Michael J. Ainscough warns, "To the bio-weaponeer, these are essentially blueprints that would enable him to make microorganisms more harmful."[43]

Still another new threat consists of what scientists call stealth viruses. These are genetically engineered viruses that enter the cells of a human host and remain dormant for a while. At a signal sent by the biological attacker, however, the virus will suddenly become active and rapidly kill the host. "As a biological weapon," Ainscough points out, "a stealth virus could [secretly] infect the genome [DNA blueprints] of a population. Later, the virus could be activated in the targeted population, or a threat of activation could be used as blackmail."[44]

The natural question is: How will nations and peoples deal with these new and frightening challenges, as well as with existing biological warfare challenges? More specifically, how can these threats be prevented in the first place? Although there is no single or simple answer to these questions, various scientists, military strategists, politicians, and other experts have offered suggestions. Among them are stricter adherence to international conventions banning the use of weapons of mass destruction, the use of nuclear weapons as a counterthreat to bioweapons, improving biodefenses through medical and technical advances, and setting strong moral standards for all nations and individuals to follow.

Improving the BWC by Adding a Special Protocol

In regard to international conventions and protocols, the major nations of the world have been legally bound by the articles of the BWC since 1972, the year it officially went into effect. This does not mean, however, that all the signers of the convention obeyed the rules and refrained from making new biological weapons. In fact, evidence later revealed that the Soviet Union and other nations broke the treaty's rules and continued to produce bioweapons in secret. As a result, a number of national leaders and expert observers came to view the BWC as basically useless.

Yet some of these critics recognized that the BWC and other such international agreements retained at least the potential for reducing the creation of weapons of mass destruction. The

Botulinum toxin is tested in a lab. How to handle such materials and the threat of biological warfare is debated.

problem, the critics pointed out, was that the BWC lacked provisions for enforcing its will; in other words, the signers of the treaty could not legally force a suspected rule breaker to allow international inspections and investigations of its labs and other facilities. In the 1990s, therefore, a group of diplomats from several countries began drawing up a special enforcement protocol they hoped to add to the BWC. Completed in April 2001, the protocol provides for a unit of inspectors to monitor the biological research activities of BWC members.

Several countries declared their willingness to sign the new protocol. However, the United States, the world's sole superpower, refused to sign. The Bush administration claimed it could not accept

Pakistani policemen stand guard outside government offices. Although the government of Pakistan expressed objections to new biological weapons rules, it did not reject them outright.

the protocol because the rules set forth in the document are too weak to catch potential cheaters. Both the administration and supporters of its rejection of the protocol also said that some of the provisions of the document might reveal vital military secrets and this could potentially pose a risk to U.S. national security.

Those critical of the U.S. refusal to accept the new protocol point to what they view as the document's potential benefits. They also say that the refusal makes the United States look less reasonable than several nations widely viewed as rogue states. "The protocol complements intelligence sources, diplomacy, and military power," states the Council for a Livable World (CLW), an American lobbying group that strongly supports international arms controls.

> The protocol also enhances the fight against bio-terrorism as it works to prevent proliferation of biological weapons. . . . The protocol is a protective step in defending our nation. . . . The BWC Protocol strengthens the convention's requirement to encourage scientific and technical cooperation to work for the prevention of disease and for peaceful purposes. . . . Finally, among its Western allies . . . the United States stood alone in its re-

jection of the [protocol] and took a stance more extreme than those taken by Cuba, . . . Libya, Pakistan, and Iran, all of which voiced their objections to the [protocol's] text but never formally rejected it.[45]

Can Nuclear Deterrence Prevent Biological Warfare?

Some of the same experts and observers who oppose U.S. acceptance of the BWC Protocol think that at least some future biological attacks may be prevented by nuclear deterrence. In other words, someone may refrain from launching a biological attack out of fear of nuclear retaliation. Experts caution that this kind of deterrence will likely work mainly in the specific case of rogue nations rather

Should the United States Withdraw from the BWC?

Although many experts feel that international protocols and conventions are useful tools for preventing the spread of biological weapons, others disagree. Here, Dave Kopel of the Independence Institute and Glenn Reynolds of the University of Tennessee argue that the United States should withdraw entirely from the 1972 Biological Warfare Convention.

The United States ought to realize that the Biological Warfare Convention is a proven failure, having already induced the creation of massive stockpiles of sophisticated bio-war agents by the Soviet Union, stockpiles that remain available for terrorists or anyone else who can get hold of them. . . . The BWC was a well-intentioned mistake by people who mistook peace agreements for peace itself. . . . Who knows what other countries have followed the Soviet lead and today are producing bio-war weapons because the BWC guarantees that the United States can't fight fire with fire [by making its own biological weapons]?

Dave Kopel and Glenn Reynolds, "Another Bad Treaty," *National Review Online*. September 6, 2001. www.national review.com/kopel/kopel090601.shtml.

than that of individual terrorists or terrorist groups. The latter will probably not be deterred by a nuclear threat because they do not usually represent or act on the orders of an organized nation. Yet these individuals and groups often hide out inside established countries. They do this partly because they know that the United States and other nations that possess nuclear arms will not use them to kill tens of thousands of innocent citizens of those countries in order to kill a handful of international criminals.

A rogue nation-state, on the other hand, may be fair game for a nuclear response if it is proven to be behind a deadly attack on another country. And the leader or leaders of such a state may think twice about launching biological weapons against a nuclear power such as the United States, Russia, Britain, or Israel. In fact, this is exactly what happened when Iraqi dictator Saddam Hussein decided not to launch bioweapons against U.S. troops who were conducting a police action against his country in 1991.

The Need for Coordination

Defending against biological weapons attacks requires us to further sharpen our policy, coordination, and planning to integrate the biodefense capabilities that reside at the federal, state, and private sector levels.

George W. Bush, "Biodefense for the 21st Century," The White House, April 28, 2004. www.whitehouse.gov/homeland/20040430.html.

Although Saddam backed down out of fear of nuclear weapons, it is impossible to predict whether the leaders of other rogue nations will do the same in the future. Nevertheless, some experts say that the United States should keep the threat of nuclear retaliation as a sort of trump card against potential future biological attacks by rogue nations such as Iran and North Korea. According to David G. Gompert, head of the National Security Research Division of the RAND Corporation:

> While it is possible to imagine a biological attack that would not warrant a nuclear response, this is no reason to discard

A U.S. soldier takes part in an exercise during the 1991 Gulf War. During that war, Saddam Hussein used conventional rather than biological weapons.

the option of a nuclear response against any and all possible biological attacks. When thousands of Soviet nuclear weapons were poised to strike, the first use of nuclear weapons by the United States risked a general nuclear cataclysm. In contrast, U.S. nuclear retaliation for a biological attack by a rogue state would risk, at worst, another [biological or chemical] attack—awful to be sure, but worth the risk in order to deter biological use in the first place. More likely, having proven its resolve with a presumably selective nuclear detonation, the United States would deter further escalation and prevail.[46]

Those who disagree with this position worry about unnecessary nuclear proliferation. They say that if the few existing nuclear powers begin using their nuclear bombs to deter biological or chemical attacks, many other nations will decide they need nuclear weapons for the same purpose. "Nuclear deterrence is ill-suited to protecting the United States and its interests against . . . biological attacks," former U.S. diplomat Thomas Graham Jr. declares,

> and to employ it in this fashion would make the spread of nuclear weapons much more likely. We can deter and respond to . . . biological weapons in a manner fully protective of our national security; we cannot assure our national security in a world armed to the teeth with nuclear weapons.[47]

Medical and Technical Steps and Advancements

Both signing international conventions and threatening to use nuclear weapons against bioterrorists might be thought of as political means of preventing the future use of bioweapons. Yet some experts contend that these approaches are generalized and potentially unreliable. More specific, reliable, and provably effective, they say, would be medical and technical steps and advancements with clear, measurable results. For example, some experts have called for the destruction of all surviving smallpox samples so that the possibility of these samples, or small parts of them, falling into the hands of rogue nations or terrorists would be eliminated. At present, however, no definite plans for destroying these potentially deadly cultures have been proposed by the major members of the international community.

Another medical-technical avenue toward preventing biological warfare is using available scientific resources to strengthen national and international biodefenses. One way this might be done, several scientists say, is to step up ongoing efforts to understand the nature of the human genome, the DNA blueprints of life. According to this view, such research will eventually demonstrate exactly what happens in a human cell when it is infected with a disease germ or dangerous toxin. Then it will be possible to design defensive strategies on a microscopic level that will be able to boost the body's immune system and thereby nullify the destructive effects of a biological attack.

Nuclear Weapons Will Not Deter Biological Warfare

General Lee Butler, former commander of the U.S. Strategic Air Command, argues that any faith that nuclear weapons will deter the use of biological weapons is misplaced.

Sad to say, the Cold War lives on in the minds of those who cannot let go the fears, beliefs, and the enmities born of the nuclear age. What better illustration of misplaced faith in nuclear deterrence than the persistent belief that the retaliation with nuclear weapons is a legitimate and appropriate response to post–Cold War threats posed by biological . . . weapons of mass destruction. . . . What could possibly justify our resorting to the very means we properly abhor and condemn? . . . Would we hold an entire society accountable for the decision of a single demented leader? . . . It is wrong in every aspect. It is wrong politically. It makes no sense militarily. And morally, in my view, it is indefensible.

Lee Butler, "The Case Against Nuclear Deterrence," *Disarmament Times*, April 1998.

Concurrent with these studies of cells and genes, a number of scientists say, will be the development of new vaccines. It would be preferable to develop special vaccines that could work against a broad range of infections rather than having one vaccine for each disease. This is because no one can be sure of the identity of a disease spread in a biological attack until many people are already sick. A vaccine that works against multiple diseases would offer a broader range of protection for a larger portion of the population.

On a more logistical level, a number of experts say that simply providing more government funding would allow the building of more and better lab facilities. At present, they say, not enough labs in the United States and other Western countries are equipped with the latest devices for recognizing and culturing some of the germs that rogue states or terrorists might use in an attack. At the same time, these experts say, existing computer databases should be expanded to provide support in diagnosing and treating diseases released by attackers.

Still another logistical, hands-on approach to improving biodefenses would be to make special high-tech suits that would completely shield first responders and others from deadly germs and toxins. Although biohazard suits have been in use for several

Improved biohazard suits will automatically seal themselves after being punctured.

years, these outfits suffer from a major disadvantage—if a suit is punctured, microbes can enter and infect the wearer. What is needed is a suit that automatically seals itself if it is punctured. Such suits could also be put on already infected people to keep them from spreading the disease to health-care workers and other citizens. The same special material used in making such a suit could also be used in a more localized patch that would isolate a skin wound from biological agents or other contaminants.

A Peaceful Purpose

Perhaps the most effective way for the United States to build international confidence in the peaceful nature of its biodefense program would be for the president to make a public statement renouncing the prospective development of genetically modified microorganisms.

Jonathon B. Tucker, "Biological Threat Assessment: Is the Cure Worse than the Disease?" *Arms Control Today*, October 2004.

Until recently, biohazard suits and skin patches with these advanced capabilities existed only in science fiction movies. But in 2004 West Virginia inventor Jeremy McGowan patented the prototype of the Biodressing. The full name of the invention is Wound Dressing Impervious to Chemical and Biological Agents. According to one description of this revolutionary device:

> The biodressing is designed to cover a wound and the adhesive border is designed to adhere to skin surrounding a wound, thereby containing bodily fluids within the dressing, while preventing chemical or biological agents from entering the wound. . . . It would be a significant advancement in the treatment of persons wounded in a . . . biologically contaminated environment to be treated with a wound dressing capable of rapidly providing a sealed wound environment . . . while patching any damage to the chemical and biological protective garment. It would also be a significant advance . . . [by] preventing attending persons from exposure to . . . contagions and pathogens.[48]

A mail handler wears gloves to protect against possible anthrax exposure.

Will Moral Restraints Prevent Future Bioweapons Attacks?

Some modern observers have concluded that although such technical advances are valuable as precautions, they will never be needed in any significant quantities. According to this view, any future biological attacks will be like those perpetrated by the Rashneeshees and whoever placed anthrax spores in letters in 2001. In other words, such attacks will be random and small scale, and will result in few or no deaths. According to this view, large-scale biological attacks will be unlikely because ultimately those capable of engineering such major events will recognize the moral repugnance of biological mass murder.

An often-cited example of this moral dimension of the issue is the development of biological weapons by the United States, Britain, the Soviet Union, and other nations during the twentieth century. Although these countries clearly possessed the means to launch biological attacks on one another, they did not do so. Even the Soviets, widely seen as international rule breakers, refrained from using their vast biological stockpiles. Some people assume that moral restraints—certain deep-seated human taboos and inhibitions against mass murder—were involved.

However, those who disagree with this view point out that another nation that developed biological weapons in the twentieth century—Japan—did actually use them, against the Chinese. Moreover, the stockpiling and even the use of biological weapons by nation-states may, over time, seem expected and necessary rather than morally unacceptable. "If the number of biological weapons programs throughout the world continues to grow," Cole theorizes,

> biological arsenals may come to be seen as normal. The moral sense of repugnance about these weapons could become compromised. . . . If such weapons are in stock [in large numbers around the world], even the most ethically sensitive nation might use them as a last resort. A desperate parent might [illegally] buy an organ for a child; [similarly,] a nation facing devastation might use repugnant weaponry if available.[49]

Critics of the moral restraint argument also point out that even if the leaders and scientists of nation-states exhibit such restraints, it is unlikely that renegade terrorist groups and individual terrorists will do so. As Yale University scholar Martin Shubik puts it:

> It is a safe bet that, as the [biological] weaponry becomes cheaper and requires fewer individuals for delivery, a threshold will be reached where there will be enough socially alienated, mad, or fanatical individuals to break taboos or overcome the inhibitions.[50]

Reasonable Steps to Prevent a Horrible Future

If the critics are right and moral restraints can no longer be counted on to prevent the use of weapons of mass destruction, including biological ones, what reasonable steps can be taken to prevent a biological holocaust? Can the promotion and enforcement of international protocols, increased funding for biodefenses, and the development of new medical and technological tools be supplemented by other approaches?

Shubik and other experts offer a few more practical suggestions. First, they say, U.S. police and investigative agencies, such as the FBI and CIA, need to share more information and coordinate more effectively with one another. This will aid efforts to catch potential bioterrorists before they strike. Also, many expert observers call for more comprehensive studies that show what makes certain individuals become alienated from society and willing to commit mass murder for a cause. If such psychological aspects of the problem are better understood, ways might be found to channel the negative energies of such people into more constructive pursuits. Some experts also call for programs in which rich nations like the United States would take steps to end mass poverty and ignorance around the world. Supposedly this would greatly reduce the number of people who feel disaffected and helpless and who might resort to terrorism to vent their anger and despair. Increasing public awareness of the bioweapons threat will also be an important tool in the effort to avert biological attacks.

The Biological Century?

Clearly, all of these steps and approaches, as well as ones yet to be conceived, will be needed to combat biological warfare in the future. One thing that nearly all of the scientists and other experts agree on is that the threat is real and imminent. As time goes on, biological weapons will likely be increasingly used as weapons of choice by rogue nations and terrorists. Ainscough delivers a prophecy that is disturbing but must, he says, be taken seriously by concerned people everywhere:

Government officials prepare to testify at a Senate hearing on worldwide threats, including the threat of biological warfare.

The twentieth century was dominated by physics, but recent breakthroughs indicate that the next one hundred years likely will be "the biological century." There are those who say "the First World War was chemical; the Second World War was nuclear; and that the Third World War—God forbid—will be biological."[51]

Introduction: Biological Weapons: Knowledge, Intent, and Morality

1. Leonard A. Cole, *The Eleventh Plague: The Politics of Biological and Chemical Warfare.* New York: W. H. Freeman, 2001, pp. 219–20.

2. Cole, *Eleventh Plague*, p. 221.

3. Jim A. Davis, "A Biological Warfare Wake-Up Call: Prevalent Myths and Likely Scenarios," in *The Gathering Biological Warfare Storm,* ed. Jim A. Davis and Barry R. Schneider. London: Praeger, 2004, p. 191.

Chapter 1: Biological Agents and Their Harmful Effects

4. Eric Croddy, *Chemical and Biological Warfare: A Comprehensive Survey for the Concerned Citizen.* New York: Copernicus, 2002, pp. 67–68.

5. Croddy, *Chemical and Biological Warfare*, p. 68.

6. Brenda J. McEleney, "Smallpox: A Primer," *The Gathering Biological Warfare Storm*, ed. Jim A Davis and Barry R. Schneider. London: Praeger, 2004, pp. 92–93.

7. McEleney, "Smallpox," p. 99.

8. Cole, *Eleventh Plague*, p. 160.

9. Croddy, *Chemical and Biological Warfare*, p. 216.

10. Michael E. Peterson, "Agro-Terrorism and Foot-and-Mouth Disease: Is the United States Prepared?" in *The Gathering Biological Warfare Storm*, ed. Jim A. Davis and Barry R. Schneider. London: Praeger, 2004, p. 14.

Chapter 2: The Threat of Existing Bioweapons Programs

11. Dee Ann Divis and Nicholas M. Horrock, "Living in Terror, Part I: Deadly Laboratories," United Press International, July 2, 2003.

12. "Convention on the Prohibition of the Development, Production and Stockpiling of Bacteriological (Biological) and Toxin Weapons and on Their Destruction," Biological and Toxin Weapons Convention Web site. www.opbw.org/convention/conv.html.

13. Croddy, *Chemical and Biological Warfare*, p. 35.

14. Wendy Orent, "After Anthrax," *Amercian Prospect*, May 8, 2000.

15. Quoted in Orent, "After Anthrax," p. 7.

16. Quoted in Croddy, *Chemical and Biological Warfare*, p. 52.

17. Tara O'Toole and Donald A. Henderson, "A Clearly Present Danger," *Harvard International Review* 23 (Fall 2001): 51.

Chapter 3: The Increasing and Daunting Threat of Bioterrorism

18. Frank J. Cilluffo, testimony before the U.S. Senate Committee on Foreign Relations, September 5, 2001.

19. Barry R. Schneider, "U.S. Biodefense Readiness: Thoughts After September 11," in *The Gathering Biological Warfare Storm*, ed. Jim A. Davis and Barry R. Schneider. London: Praeger, 2004. p. 1.

20. Cilluffo, testimony.

21. Jim A. Davis and Anna Winegar, "The Anthrax Terror: DOD's Number One Biological Threat," in *The Gathering Biological Warfare Storm*, ed. Jim A. Davis and Barry R. Schneider. London: Praeger, 2004, p. 57.

22. Croddy, *Chemical and Biological Warfare*, p. 9.

23. Jessica Stern, "The Prospects for Domestic Bio-Terror," *Emerging Infectious Diseases* 5 (July/August 1999): 521.

24. Stern, "Prospects for Domestic Bio-Terror," p. 522.

25. Anne Kohnen, "Responding to the Threat of Bio-Terrorism: Specific Recommendations for the U.S. Department of Agriculture," *ESDP Discussion Paper 2000–2004.* Cambridge, MA: Kennedy School of Government, October 2000, p. 12.

26. Davis, "A Biological Warfare Wake-Up Call," p. 201.

Chapter 4: Building Up Defenses Against Biological Attacks

27. Schneider, "U.S. Biodefense Readiness," pp. 4–5.

28. Peterson, "Agro-Terrorism," p. 23.

29. Peterson, "Agro-Terrorism," p. 24.

30. Quoted in William Dudley, *Biological Warfare: Opposing Viewpoints.* San Diego: Greenhaven, 2004, pp. 107–108.

31. Quoted in John Mintz, "Bio-Terror's War Game Shows Lack of Readiness," *Washington Post*, January 15, 2005, p. A12.

32. David Stripp, "Bio-Terror is in the Air," *Fortune*, October 15, 2001, p. 151.

33. Barbara F. Bullock, "Surveillance and Detection: A Public Health Response to Bio-Terrorism," in *The Gathering Biological Warfare Storm*, ed. Jim A. Davis and Barry R. Schneider. London: Praeger, 2004, pp. 34–35.

34. Schneider, "U.S. Biodefense Readiness," p. 4.

35. Croddy, *Chemical and Biological Warfare*, p. 69.

36. Louis Warren, "Before It's Too Late, Vaccinate Against Bio-Terror," *Los Angeles Times*, October 1, 2001, p. B11.

37. Steven Black, "Smallpox Sense," December 24, 2001. www.vaccinationnews.com/DailyNews/December2001/Small poxSense.htm.

38. Lawrence O. Gostin, "Yes, New Laws Are Needed to Enable State and Federal Agencies to Work Together in an Emergency," *Insight on the News*, January 7, 2002.

39. Shannon Brownlee, "Under Control—Why America Isn't Ready for Bioterrorism," *New Republic*, October 29, 2001.

40. Twila Brase, "A Model for Medical Tyranny," *Ideas on Liberty*, August 2002.

41. Benjamin Franklin, "Pennsylvania Assembly: Reply to Governor, November 11, 1755," in *The Papers of Benjamin Franklin*, vol. 6, ed. Leonard W. Laboree. New Haven, CT: Yale University Press, 1963, p. 242.

Chapter 5: Preventing Future Biological Weapons Threats

42. Malcolm R. Dando, *The New Biological Weapons: Threat, Proliferation, and Control.* Boulder, CO: Lynne Rienner, 2001, p. 11.

43. Michael J. Ainscough, "New Generation Bio-Weapons: Genetic Engineering and Biological Warfare," in *The Gathering Biological Warfare Storm*, ed. Jim A. Davis and Barry R. Schneider. London: Praeger, 2004, p. 178.

44. Ainscough, "New Generation Bio-weapons," p. 180.

45. Council for a Livable World, "Biological Weapons Convention," November 2002. www.clw.org/archive/control/bwc.html.

46. David E. Gompert, "Sharpen the Fear," *Bulletin of the Atomic Scientists*, January/February 2000, p. 76.

47. Thomas Graham Jr., "Nuclear Targeting and the Role of Nuclear Weapons," *Defense News*, February 23–March 1, 1998.

48. "Biodresssing." www.answers.com/topic/biodressing.

49. Cole, *Eleventh Plague*, pp. 222–23.

50. Martin Shubik, "Terrorism, Technology, and the Socioeconomics of Death," *Comparative Strategy* 16, no. 4 (1997): 409.

51. Ainscough, "New Generation Bio-Weapons," p. 186.

Chapter 1: Biological Agents and Their Harmful Effects

1. What two major factors must a would-be biological attacker consider in choosing a biological agent to use as a weapon?

2. What are the symptoms of bubonic plague?

3. What could a nation or terrorist group hope to accomplish by culturing foot-and-mouth disease microbes and unleashing them in an enemy's homeland?

Chapter 2: The Threat of Existing Bioweapons Programs

1. What proved to be some of the weaknesses of the Geneva Protocol, which sought to eradicate biological weapons?

2. Describe two accidents involving dangerous biological agents produced by state-sponsored bioweapons programs.

3. Which potentially lethal biological agents did Iraq's "Doctor Germ" admit to producing in the 1990s?

Chapter 3: The Increasing and Daunting Threat of Bioterrorism

1. Describe what occurred in the 1984 Rashneeshee biological attack.

2. List at least four reasons why bioweapons are increasingly becoming weapons of choice for foreign terrorists.

3. What are three potential advantages for individuals who choose to launch an agroterrorist assault?

Chapter 4: Building Up Defenses Against Biological Attacks

1. Identify APHIS and READEO. What do these organizations do?

2. Describe the unfolding scenario and final outcome of Operation Dark Winter.

3. What arguments do critics of mass vaccinations use to support their view that such programs are unnecessary and potentially dangerous?

Chapter 5: Preventing Future Biological Weapons Threats

1. Describe three technical advances in biology and biotechnology that will likely cause the creation of more sophisticated biological weapons in the future.

2. Cite the main arguments both for and against the United States and other nuclear powers using their nuclear weapons in hopes of deterring potential biological attacks by rogue nations.

3. What factors suggest to many experts that moral restraints against mass murder can no longer be counted on to deter certain countries, groups, or individuals from launching biological attacks?

FOR MORE INFORMATION

Books

Leonard A. Cole, *The Eleventh Plague: The Politics of Biological and Chemical Warfare.* New York: W.H. Freeman, 2001. A instructive and interesting study of the way various nations have recently been dealing with the emerging threat of biological warfare.

William Dudley, ed., *Biological Warfare: Opposing Viewpoints.* San Diego: Greenhaven, 2004. A very well-chosen and informative collection of articles about the issue of biological weapons and how their use by terrorists might be averted.

Stephen Endicott and Edward Hagerman, *The United States and Biological Warfare: Secrets from the Early Cold War and Korea.* Bloomington: Indiana University Press, 1999. Tells how the United States conducted research into biological weapons, subsequently renouncing these efforts during the administration of President Richard Nixon.

Jeanne Guillemin, *Anthrax: The Investigation of a Deadly Outbreak.* Berkeley and Los Angeles: University of California Press, 1999. A highly detailed account of the deadly outbreak of anthrax that struck the Soviet Union in 1979.

Tahara Hasan, *Anthrax Attacks Around the World.* New York: Rosen, 2003. This well-written volume looks at all of the terrorist incidents involving anthrax to date.

Robert Hutchinson, *Weapons of Mass Destruction: The No-Nonsense Guide to Nuclear, Chemical and Biological Weapons Today.* London: Weidenfeld & Nicolson, 2003. A thoughtful look at the various kinds of weapons, including biological ones, that pose a serious threat to global peace and security.

Judith Miller, Stephen Engelberg, and William Broad, *Germs: Biological Weapons and America's Secret War.* New York: Simon & Schuster, 2001. A riveting account of the developing threat of biological warfare in recent decades, including the little-publicized 1984 biological attack on an Oregon town by a local cult.

Don Nardo, *Germs.* San Diego: Lucent, 2003. A useful general overview of the many different kinds of germs, including both harmful ones and beneficial ones.

Clay I. Neff, *Biological Weapons.* San Diego: Greenhaven, 2005. A useful collection of insights into the issue of biological warfare and the potential harm it may do to humanity in the near future.

Tom Ridgway, *Smallpox.* New York: Rosen Publishing, 2001. An up-to-date synopsis of the history of one of the worst diseases in history.

Web Sites

BiodefenseEducation.org (www.biodefenseeducation.org). The site sums itself up this way: "BiodefenseEducation.org is an [online] library . . . intended to serve as a source of continuing education on biodefense, bioterrorism and biological warfare." Contains many links to useful articles about deadly germs, their potential uses as weapons, vaccines to combat them, and so on.

Biological Warfare, Wikipedia (http://en.wikipedia.org/wiki/Biologicalwarfare). An excellent starting point for those interested in the subject, with a comprehensive overview and many links to sites with supplementary information.

How Biological and Chemical Warfare Works (http://science.howstuffworks.com/biochem-war.htm). Aimed at those with little knowledge in the subject, this site offers a number of links to pages with useful information stated in easy-to-read language.

ORGANIZATIONS TO CONTACT

Center for Biosecurity of UPMC

Pier IV Bldg., 621 E. Pratt St., Suite 210, Baltimore, MD 21202

(443) 573-3304

Fax: (443) 573-3305

www.upmc-biosecurity.org

The Center for Biosecurity is an independent organization affiliated with the University of Pittsburgh Medical Center (UPMC). The Center for Biosecurity studies the current state of biological weapons and works to reduce their development and use. It also tries to develop measures to reduce the harmful effects of biological warfare, should it occur.

Centers for Disease Control and Prevention (CDC)

1600 Clifton Rd., Atlanta, GA 30333

(800) 311-3435

www.cdc.gov

The CDC is a U.S. government agency that protects the public health by preventing and controlling diseases and by responding to public health emergencies, including potential biological attacks by terrorists. Information about biological warfare agents can be obtained on the CDC's Web site.

Jane's Information Group

110 N. Royal St., Suite 200, Alexandria, VA 22314

(703) 683-3700

Fax: (703) 836-0297

www.janes.com

Jane's Information Group is a leading authority on national defense and security issues. Jane's provides current information, including articles by a wide range of experts.

Sunshine Project
101 W. Sixth St., Suite 607, Austin, TX 78701
(512) 494-0545
www.sunshine-project.org
The Sunshine Project is an international organization that examines the dangers of new weapons based on advances in biotechnology. The organization conducts research and issues periodic reports that are available on its Web site.

INDEX

agrowarfare, 13, 54–56

Ainscough, Michael J., 76, 88–89

Alibeck, Kenneth, 36–37

Animal and Plant Health Inspection Service (APHIS), 61–63

anthrax, 11
  disease cycle of, 13, 14
  pulmonary form of, 14–15, 16
  2001 attacks with, 45–46
  vaccine for, 69–70

Aum Shinrikyo, 44–45, 53

Bin Laden, Osama, 10, 42

biodressing, 85

biohazard suits, 84–85

biological agent(s)
  definition of, 11
  need for laboratories to detect, 68–69, 83–84
  as weapon, 12–13

biological warfare
  as deterrent, 86-87
  defensive measures against, 58–59, 88
  emergency responses to
    civil rights and, 74
    role of health care personnel in, 66–69
  role of public health laws, 72–74
  testing of, 63–66

future threat of, 88–89

history of, 6

moral arguments to ban, 8-9

nuclear deterrence of, 79–82
  argument against, 83

small-scale use of, 7

use of
  in World War I, 28
  in World War II, 29

Biological Warfare Convention (BWC), 33, 35
  special protocol proposed for, 77–78
  U.S. withdrawal from, argument for, 79
  violations of, 35–36, 76

biological weapons, binary, 75–76

bioterrorism, 26
  domestic, threat of, 50–53
  incidents of, 44–47

bioweapons programs, state-sponsored, attempts to ban, 32–33
  in Britain, 30–31
  in Iraq, 38–39
  in North Korea, 40–41
  in Soviet Union, 29–30

in United States, 30, 32
Black, Steven, 71, 72, 73
Black Death, 6
 see also bubonic plague
botulinum toxin, 20–22
botulism, 21
Brase, Twila, 64, 74
Brokaw, Tom, 45
Brownlee, Shannon, 73
bubonic plague, 6, 19–20
Bullock, Barbara F., 67–68
Bush, George W., 47
 on biodefense, 80

Central Intelligence Agency
 (CIA), secret biodefense
 research by, 38
Cihak, Robert C., 68
Cilluffo, Frank J., 43, 47,
 50
Clinton, Bill, 53
Cole, Leonard A., 8, 22, 87
Conant, Eve, 30
Council for a Livable World
 (CLW), 78
Croddy, Eric, 14, 16, 35–36,
 70

Dark Winter Operation, 65
Daschle, Tom, 45
Davis, Jim A., 10, 49, 57
DeMier, Mark, 65
Department of Defense, 75
Divis, Dee Ann, 27

Easterbrook, Gregg, 57
Emergency Broadcast System
 (EBS), 60

foot-and-mouth disease,
 24–25
foreign animal disease (FAD),
 60
 defense against, 61–63
Franklin, Benjamin, 74

Geneva Protocol, 33
Goldstein, Steve, 25
Gompert, David G., 80
Gong, E.J., 16
Gostin, Lawrence O., 73
Graham, Thomas, Jr., 82
Great Britain, 30–31
Gutterl, Fred, 30

Hammond, Edward, 38
Harris, Larry Wayne, 53
Henderson, Donald, 41
Hussein, Saddam, 38, 56, 80

Inglesby, Thomas, 64

Japan, 29
Jenner, Edward, 17
Johnson, Thomas J., 48

Koch, Robert, 13
Kohnen, Ann, 54, 55

Larsen, Randy, 65
Leahy, Patrick, 45
Lovell, Stanley P., 32

Markov, Georgi, 48
McEleney, Brenda J., 16–17
McGowan, Jeremy, 85
McVeigh, Timothy, 8, 50

morality
  bans on bioweapons and,
    8–9
  as deterrent, 86–87

National Warning System
  (NAWAS), 60
Nixon, Richard, 33
North Korea, bioweapons
  programs in, 40–41

Operation Dark Winter, 65
Orent, Wendy, 36
O'Toole, Tara, 41, 64

Peterson, Michael E., 25,
  61–62, 63

al Qaeda, 42
Q fever, 22–23

racism, 51–52
Rashneeshees, 44
Red Army Faction, 44
Regional Emergency Animal
  Disease Eradication
  Organization, 62–63
religion, 51–52
Reynolds, Glenn, 79
ricin, 23–24
  assassination using, 48
Russia, 36–38

saxitoxin, 23, 24
Scardaville, Michael, 66
Schneider, Barry R., 46,
  59–60, 69
September 11 attacks

(2001), 54
Shubik, Martin, 87, 88
Slueck, Michael A., 68
smallpox
  destruction of samples of, 82
  eradication of, 18–19
  exercises simulating attack
    with, 65–66
  mass vaccination against, 18
    argument against, 68,
      71–72
    argument for, 66, 70
  symptoms/spreading of,
    16–17
  vaccine, safety of, 71, 73
Soviet Union, violation of
  Biological Warfare
  Convention by, 35–36
Stern, Jessica, 51, 53
Stripp, David, 66
Symbionese Liberation Army,
  52

Taha, Rihab Rashid, 39
terrorists
  bioweapons and, 49–50
  motives of, 47
Tucker, Jonathon, B., 85

United States
  bioweapons program of, 30,
    32
  BWC and, 77–78, 79
  impact of biological attack
    on, 43–44
  overseas forces of, 56–57
  as prime target of
    bioterrorism, 53–54

ratification of Geneva
Protocol by, 33

vaccines/vaccination, 69–72
mass, against smallpox, 18
argument against, 68,
71–72
argument for, 66, 70

smallpox, safety of, 71, 73

warning systems, 60
World Health Organization
(WHO), 18
Wound Dressing Impervious
to Chemical and Biological
Agents, 85

PICTURE CREDITS

ABOUT THE AUTHOR

In addition to his numerous acclaimed volumes on ancient civilizations, historian Don Nardo has published several studies of modern scientific discoveries, phenomena, and issues. Among these are *Ice Ages*, *Ozone*, *Vaccines*, *The Extinction of the Dinosaurs*, *Cloning*, *Black Holes*, and a biography of Charles Darwin. Mr. Nardo lives with his wife, Christine, in Massachusetts.